Numbers & 1ˢᵗ Corinthians

Read the Bible Again for the First Time

Echoes Bible

Volume IV

2025

World English Bible (WEB)

Echoesbible.com

Numbers & 1 Corinthians
Read the Bible Again for the First Time
Echoes Bible, Volume IV, 2025

© 2025 Echoes Bible Foundation

The Echoes Bible Foundation is a non-profit Christian ministry dedicated to the discovery, dissemination, education and application of literary connections between the inspired books of the Bible. It is organized as a U.S. based 501(c)3.

Echoes Bible Foundation
13359 North Highway 183
Suite 406-679
Austin, Texas 78750
publish@echoesbible.org

Paul, the Apostle to the Gentiles, first acknowledged Jesus as the Messiah as a result of encountering him on the road to Damascus. Prior to that he had been known as Saul, a learned leader among the Pharisee sect of Judaism in 1st century Judea, a student of the revered rabbi Gamaliel. His thinking and imagination had been shaped by deep acquaintance with the Torah, Wisdom Literature, and Prophets (Tanakh), what Christians in the modern age generally call "the Old Testament." How, exactly, did his biblically shaped mind and soul guide his composition of his letters? The quotations from scripture are clear enough, but in ten years of study, we have discovered in the text echoes of the Old Testament structure, theme, and vocabulary in Paul's letters. In this volume, we will explore those echoes between the book of Numbers and the First Epistle to the Corinthians.

Dedication:
To Paul the Apostle

ISBN Paperback: 978-1-970720-00-6
Cover Design by Stephen Douglas Alexander, Layout by Echoes Bible Foundation

1. Christianity. 2 Bibles. 3. Bible Commentary. 4. Bible Study. 5. Old Testament. 6. New Testament.
I. Echoes Bible Foundation
II. Numbers & 1 Corinthians. Read the Bible Again for the First Time. Echoes Bible. Volume IV. 2025.

INTRODUCTION

Upon receiving the revelation from God on the road to Damascus, Paul's entire world was turned upside down. A zealous student of the Torah, having studied under Gamaliel (Acts 22:3), Paul would then spend about three years in Arabia and Damascus before going up to Jerusalem to meet Peter and James (Gal. 1:18–19). His time in Arabia must have included extended periods of revisiting the Torah, seeking to understand how he could have missed the work of Christ Jesus within it. How fascinating it would have been to sit beside Paul, to converse with him, as he began reading the Torah anew in the light of Christ. In Arabia, Paul would have started to perceive how Christ was inextricably present in every book, every story, every paragraph, and perhaps even every verse that he had studied so intently for so many years. Given God's call to him on the road to Damascus (Acts 26:17), Paul must also have re-read the Torah with an eye toward discerning God's plan to bring the Gentiles into a saving knowledge of Jesus Christ.

When Paul was set apart for ministry, he experienced the joy of sharing the Gospel directly with both Jew and Gentile. After establishing assemblies in various locations, he would then write letters to them. The New Testament preserves more than a dozen of these letters, now recognized as the inspired Word of God. Paul wrote in Greek, and when quoting the Old Testament, he necessarily did so in Greek as well, and his direct quotations are numerous. At times he also addressed topics by appealing to principle rather than direct quotation. With great conviction he affirms that "every Scripture is inspired by God and profitable for teaching, for reproof, for correction, and for training in righteousness" (2 Tim. 3:16). Yet Paul is not an easy writer to understand. Peter himself acknowledges this in 2 Peter 3:16, observing that Paul's writings contain elements that are difficult to grasp and therefore more susceptible to being twisted.

The document you hold in your hand is likely unlike any other Bible you have encountered. The Echoes Bible Foundation asserts that this approach to reading the Scriptures is more firmly grounded than ever, for it provides additional insight into how—and from where—Paul formulated his words, anchoring his approach directly back to the inspired Word of God itself. This work enables the reader to study the books of Numbers and 1 Corinthians side by side, section by section, and to see firsthand from where part of Paul's inspiration was drawn.

Our claim is that Paul used the book of Numbers as his primary outline when addressing the church at Corinth. While Numbers certainly chronicles the forty years of Israel's wandering in the wilderness, it is more than a record of travel. It is the story of God's interaction with His people after they had received the covenant at Sinai, as they entered into the process of spiritual growth during their journeys. God poured out both love and correction upon them— directly, and through the leadership and words of Moses. The overarching purpose of Numbers is the maturation of the children of Israel, guiding them from immaturity toward maturity. In the same way, Paul's first letter to the Corinthians shares this very purpose, directed toward the assembly in Corinth and the surrounding region of Achaia.

The following table shows a sampling of some of the echoes in Numbers and how they inspired some of Paul's verses.

Numbers	1 Corinthians
1 Tribes yes, but you are part of a nation	1 One without schisms
3 I am Yahweh: For the Redemption of all firstborn	2 My only focus: Jesus Christ and him crucified
6 Priestly Blessing	4 Bless others even when being persecuted
9 The addition of the 2nd Passover	5 Christ is our *Passover*
12 Moses criticized for a Cushite Wife	7 Issues of a Believer living with an Unbeliever
13 Spies sent to go gather information	10 Paul: None of us know as we ought to know
16 Korah's rebellion: the nation takes offense	10 No temptation is without a way of escape
18 All the Levites are joined as one with the Priests	10 We who are many, are one body
21 Bronze Serpent held up, people must look or they will die	11 Paul: Lord Table unworthy manner -> sickness, death
22 Baalam – Prophecies	12 List of Spiritual Gifts – Covet to Prophesy
25 God tells Moses to speak 5 words to Phinehas: I give you my covenant of peace.	14 Paul: "in the assembly I'd rather speak 5 words with understanding than 10,000 not understood
27 Daughters of Zelophehad: bring a question	14 Paul: on women's behavior in the churches
34 God promises a physical inheritance after crossing into/through the Jordan River	15 Our body is sown perishable, but raised imperishable, thru the resurrection of the dead

This document divides Numbers and 1 Corinthians into 148 *sectional pairings*, each consisting of connections between one or more verses from the two books. Because Numbers contains more verses than 1 Corinthians, a greater number of verses from Numbers are, on average, paired with fewer verses from 1 Corinthians. These **pairings** are presented in a side-by-side format so that the reader may discern what in Numbers may have partially inspired Paul in writing his corresponding words to the 1 Corinthians. Within each **pairing**, we have also identified what we believe to be more specific connections between particular statements in Numbers and the words of Paul. We refer to these more specific, individual connections as *echoes*, and in this document we have identified more than 500 echoes.

For example, in Numbers 1:1, the phrase "**spoke to Moses**" at the beginning of the verse is paired with the phrase "**Paul, called**" in 1 Corinthians 1:1. This constitutes the first echo. Next, the words "**and Aaron**" referring to Moses' brother in Numbers 1:3, are paired with the phrase "**and our brother Sosthenes**" at the end of 1 Corinthians 1:1. This constitutes the second echo, drawing a parallel between Aaron, the brother of Moses, and Sosthenes, the brother in Christ. The use of **bold underline** does not suggest that the second echo carries greater importance than the first; it functions solely as a visual aid to allow the reader's eye to identify corresponding echoes quickly. At times, non-bold underlining is also used.

In this initial sectional pairing, a total of four echoes are identified. Of particular note, both sides of the fourth echo contain the word *called* and together reflect the broader idea of a "called congregation." These four identified echoes may not be the only echoes present; however, in a black-and-white print format we have intentionally restricted our selection to those echoes that appear in sequential order.

For example, in a sectional pairing containing six echoes, the first bolded echo in Numbers will always and only be paired with the first bolded phrase in 1 Corinthians, and so forth through the section. Moreover, while Paul generally followed the sequence of Numbers in his letter, nothing prevented him from revisiting a portion of Numbers later in his writing (see the notes after 1 Cor. 12:31), nor from summarizing a section of Numbers with a single statement (see 1 Cor. 14:40). Notes appear after many pairings to explain less obvious echoes and any exceptions in format.

The *Echoes Bible* employs the World English Bible (WEB) translation, as it is available without copyright restrictions. At the same time, we often select echoes with careful attention to the Hebrew and Greek underlying the English words, and we frequently highlight such insights in the notes. That being said, the reader is encouraged to view the identified echoes as suggested connections between two inspired texts. While our suggestions themselves are not necessarily inspired, we firmly believe that the sheer preponderance, the richness of meaning, and the poetic beauty of these echoes will, in their totality, deepen a reader's love for God's Word, heighten their awe of God, and perhaps even carry them back to the joy of their first encounter with salvation—allowing them to *read the Bible again for the first time*.

The connections between these two books are real and we believe, intentional. The inspired text of Numbers, helping to awaken Paul's vast knowledge of scripture in many other passages, overshadowed by the living work of the Holy Spirit, has resulted in the God-breathed inspired words of 1 Corinthians that we read today. Because the Word of God is inspired, we have every expectation that the Holy Spirit can speak to the reader through the Echoes Bible and reveal the truth of God's intentions in the words written by Paul.

Our vision is not that any new truth would emerge from these pairings, but rather that the echoes would further demonstrate how Paul's words are firmly anchored in the truth of all Scripture, thereby greatly reducing the potential for errors in interpretation. In agreement with Peter's warning, we likewise desire that Paul's words will no longer be twisted by "ignorant or unsettled persons."

The Echoes Bible Editing Team

Numbers 1

1 Corinthians 1

Num 1:1 Yahweh **spoke to Moses** in the wilderness of Sinai, in the Tent of Meeting, on the first day of the second month, in the second year after they had come out of the land of Egypt, saying, **2** "Take a census of all the congregation of the children of Israel, by their families, by their fathers' houses, according to the number of the names, every male, one by one, **3** from twenty years old and upward, all who are able to go out to war in Israel. You **and Aaron** shall **count them by their divisions**. **4** With you there shall be a man of every tribe, each one head of his fathers' house. **5** These are the names of the men who shall stand with you: Of Reuben: Elizur the son of Shedeur. **6** Of Simeon: Shelumiel the son of Zurishaddai. **7** Of Judah: Nahshon the son of Amminadab. **8** Of Issachar: Nethanel the son of Zuar. **9** Of Zebulun: Eliab the son of Helon. **10** Of the children of Joseph: Of Ephraim: Elishama the son of Ammihud. Of Manasseh: Gamaliel the son of Pedahzur. **11** Of Benjamin: Abidan the son of Gideoni. **12** Of Dan: Ahiezer the son of Ammishaddai. **13** Of Asher: Pagiel the son of Ochran. **14** Of Gad: Eliasaph the son of Deuel. **15** Of Naphtali: Ahira the son of Enan. **16** These are those who were called of the congregation, the princes of the tribes of their fathers; they were the heads of the thousands of Israel.

1Cor 1:1 **Paul, called** to be an apostle of Jesus Christ through the will of God, **and our brother Sosthenes,**

2 to the **assembly of God which is at Corinth**—those who are sanctified in Christ Jesus, **called saints, with all who call on the name** of our Lord Jesus Christ in every place, both theirs and ours:

3 Grace to you and peace from God our Father and the Lord Jesus Christ.

NOTE: [Bamidbar] *Bamidbar* (Hebrew name for Numbers) is divided into ten Jewish Torah portions (Parshat), the first matching the book's name. The Echoes Bible's sections align with these boundaries and are marked with brackets in the notes.

Num 1:17 Moses and Aaron took these men who are mentioned by name. **18** They assembled all the congregation together on the first day of the second month; **and they declared their ancestry by their families**, by their fathers' houses, according to the **number of the names**, from twenty years old and upward, one by one. **19** As Yahweh commanded Moses, so he counted them in the wilderness of Sinai.

1Cor 1:4 I always thank my God concerning you for the **grace of God which was given you in Christ Jesus, 5** that in everything **you were enriched in him**, in all speech and all knowledge—

NOTE: While the Children of Israel saw themselves as disadvantaged in the wilderness, God saw it differently and wanted them to see that their treasure was in the people themselves. Paul echoes this by saying that grace was already given, and that they (the believers) have already been enriched in God.

Num 1:20 The <u>children of Reuben</u>, Israel's firstborn, their generations, by their families, by their fathers' houses, according to the number of the names, one by one, every male from twenty years old and upward, all who were able to go out to war: **21** those who were counted of them, of the tribe of Reuben, were forty-six thousand five hundred.

22 Of the **children of Simeon**, their generations, by their families, by their fathers' houses, those who were counted of it, according to the number of the names, one by one, every male from twenty years old and upward, all who were able to go out to war: **23** those who were counted of them, of the tribe of Simeon, were fifty-nine thousand three hundred.

24 Of the **<u>children of Gad</u>**, their generations, by their families, by their fathers' houses, according to the number of the names, from twenty years old and upward, all who were able to go out to war: **25** those who were counted of them, of the tribe of Gad, were forty-five thousand six hundred fifty.

26 Of the **children of Judah**, their generations, by their families, by their fathers' houses, according to the number of the names, from twenty years old and upward, all who were able to go out to war: **27** those who were counted of them, of the tribe of Judah, were seventy-four thousand six hundred.

28 Of the **<u>children of Issachar</u>**, their generations, by their families, by their fathers' houses, according to the number of the names, from twenty years old and upward, all who were able to go out to war: **29** those who were counted of them, of the tribe of Issachar, were fifty-four thousand four hundred.

30 Of the **children of Zebulun**, their generations, by their families, by their fathers' houses, according to the number of the names, from twenty years old and upward, all who were able to go out to war: **31** those who were counted of them, of the tribe of Zebulun, were fifty-seven thousand four hundred.

1Cor 1:6 even as the testimony of Christ was confirmed in you— **7 <u>so that you come behind in no gift, waiting for the revelation of our Lord Jesus Christ</u>, 8** who will also **confirm you until the end, blameless in the day of our Lord Jesus Christ**. **9** God is faithful, through whom **<u>you were called into the fellowship of his Son</u>**, Jesus Christ our Lord.

10 Now I beg you, brothers, through the name of our Lord Jesus Christ, that you all **speak the same thing, and that there be no divisions among you**, but that you be **<u>perfected together in the same mind</u>** and in the **same judgment**.

NOTE: Paul must have had great knowledge about the weaknesses of each tribe and used their strengths or weaknesses to inspire his comments. For instance, we suggest an echo between the tribe of Reuben, which means "behold a son," and "coming behind in no gift" as an allusion to Jacob's charge to Reuben in Genesis 49:3 saying, "although he is the firstborn son, because of his sin, he will not have preeminence!" Paul turns this around and desires that the Corinthians not fall behind in gifts due to sin as they wait for the second coming of Christ. The tribe of Simeon was blamed by Jacob for their cruel wrath in Gen 49:7. But Paul sees God's redemptive plan for that tribe and echoes that in his future desire for the Corinthians that they be "blameless in the day of our Lord Jesus Christ." Judah, the lead tribe from which Christ would come, has responsibility to speak out against divisions. With this pattern of echoes established, we can infer Paul's thoughts about the other tribes from the parallelism. That Paul loves parallelism will be proven many times over in this document.

Num 1:32 Of the <u>**children of Joseph, of the children of Ephraim**</u>, their generations, by their families, by their fathers' houses, according to the number of the names, from twenty years old and upward, all who were able to go out to war: **33** those who were counted of them, of the tribe of Ephraim, were forty thousand five hundred.

34 Of the **children of Manasseh**, their generations, by their families, by their fathers' houses, according to the number of the names, from twenty years old and upward, all who were able to go out to war: **35** those who were counted of them, of the tribe of Manasseh, were thirty-two thousand two hundred.

36 Of the <u>**children of Benjamin**</u>, their generations, by their families, by their fathers' houses, according to the number of the names, from twenty years old and upward, all who were able to go out to war: **37** those who were counted of them, of the tribe of Benjamin, were thirty-five thousand four hundred.

38 Of the **children of Dan**, their generations, by their families, by their fathers' houses, according to the number of the names, from twenty years old and upward, all who were able to go out to war: **39** those who were counted of them, of the tribe of Dan, were sixty-two thousand seven hundred.

40 Of the <u>**children of Asher**</u>, their generations, by their families, by their fathers' houses, according to the number of the names, from twenty years old and upward, all who were able to go out to war: **41** those who were counted of them, of the tribe of Asher, were forty-one thousand five hundred.

42 Of the **children of Naphtali**, their generations, by their families, by their fathers' houses, according to the number of the names, from twenty years old and upward, all who were able to go out to war: **43** those who were counted of them, of the tribe of Naphtali, were fifty-three thousand four hundred.

1Cor 1:11 For it has been reported to me concerning you, my brothers, by those who are from <u>**Chloe's household, that there are contentions among you**</u>.

12 Now I mean this, that **each one of you says, "I follow Paul," "I follow Apollos," "I follow Cephas," or "I follow Christ."** **13** Is Christ divided? <u>**Was Paul crucified for you**</u>? Or were you baptized in the name of Paul? **14** I thank God that I **baptized none of you** except Crispus and Gaius, **15** so that <u>**no one should say that I had baptized you into my own name**</u>. **16** (I also **baptized the household of Stephanas**; besides them, I don't know whether I baptized any other.)

NOTE: God's decision to allow the younger son Ephraim to carry the higher honor within the household of Joseph, could have easily been a cause for contention. The tribe of Manasseh was the most divided tribe of all in that it was the only one physically divided into two parts on the east and west sides of the Jordan. Regarding Benjamin, the site of Christ's crucifixion is technically in the land of Benjamin, not Judah whose northern border is the Hinnom valley. In addition, Paul may have singled out himself here because Benjamin was his own tribe (Philippians 3:5). Paul's statement in 1:16b "I don't know whether I baptized any other, might be an allusion to the fact that Levi is missing from the list of tribes.

Num 1:44 These are those who were counted, whom Moses and Aaron counted, and the princes of Israel, being twelve men: they were each one for his fathers' house. **45** So all those who were counted of the children of Israel by their fathers' houses, from twenty years old and upward, all who were able to go out to war in Israel— **46** all those who were counted were **six hundred three thousand five hundred fifty**.

1Cor 1:17 For Christ sent me not to baptize, but to preach the Good News— not in wisdom of words, so that the cross of Christ **wouldn't be made void**.

NOTE: While each tribe retains its separate identity and census, the nation of Israel is counted as a whole single entity when it comes to performing the deeds of war.

Num 1:47 But the Levites after the tribe of their fathers were not counted among them. **48** For Yahweh spoke to Moses, saying, **49** "Only the tribe of Levi you shall not count, neither shall you take a census of them among the children of Israel; **50** but appoint the Levites over the **Tabernacle of the Testimony**, and over all its furnishings, and over all that belongs to it. They shall carry the tabernacle and all its furnishings; and they shall take care of it and shall encamp around it. **51** When the tabernacle is to move, the Levites shall take it down; and when the tabernacle is to be set up, the Levites shall set it up. The stranger who comes near shall be put to **death**. **52** The children of Israel shall pitch their tents, every man by his own camp, and every man by his own standard, according to their divisions. **53** But the Levites shall encamp around the Tabernacle of the Testimony, that there may be **no wrath on the congregation** of the children of Israel. The Levites shall be responsible for the Tabernacle of the Testimony." **54** Thus the children of Israel did. According to all that Yahweh commanded Moses, so they did.

1Cor 1:18 For the **word of the cross** is foolishness to those who are **dying**, but to us who are being saved it is the power of God. **19** For it is written, "**I will destroy the wisdom of the wise**. I will bring the discernment of the discerning to nothing."

Numbers 2	1 Cor. 1:20

Num 2:1 Yahweh spoke to Moses and to Aaron, saying, **2** "The children of Israel shall encamp every man by his own standard, with the banners of their fathers' houses. They shall encamp around the Tent of Meeting at a distance from it.

3 "Those who encamp on the **east side** toward the sunrise shall be of the standard of the camp of Judah, according to their divisions. The prince of the children of Judah shall be Nahshon the son of Amminadab. **4** His division, and those who were counted of them, were seventy-four thousand six hundred. **5** "Those who encamp next to him shall be the tribe of Issachar. The prince of the children of Issachar shall be Nethanel the son of Zuar. **6** His division, and those who were counted of it, were fifty-four thousand four hundred. **7** "The tribe of Zebulun: the prince of the children of Zebulun shall be Eliab the son of Helon. **8** His division, and those who were counted of it, were fifty-seven thousand four hundred. **9** "All who were counted of the camp of Judah were one hundred eighty-six thousand four hundred, according to their divisions. They shall set out first.

10 "On the **south side** shall be the standard of the camp of Reuben according to their divisions. The prince of the children of Reuben shall be Elizur the son of Shedeur. **11** His division, and those who were counted of it, were forty-six thousand five hundred. **12** "Those who encamp next to him shall be the tribe of Simeon. The prince of the children of Simeon shall be Shelumiel the son of Zurishaddai. **13** His division, and those who were counted of them, were fifty-nine thousand three hundred. **14** "The tribe of Gad: the prince of the children of Gad shall be Eliasaph the son of Reuel. **15** His division, and those who were counted of them, were forty-five thousand six hundred fifty. **16** "All who were counted of the camp of Reuben were one hundred fifty-one thousand four hundred fifty, according to their armies. They shall set out second. **17** "Then the Tent of Meeting shall set out, with the camp of the Levites in the middle of the camps. As they encamp, so shall they set out, every man in his place, by their standards."

1Cor 1:20 Where is the wise? Where is the scribe? Where is the debater of this age? Hasn't God made foolish the wisdom of this world? **21** For seeing that in the wisdom of God, the world through its wisdom didn't know God, it was God's good pleasure through the foolishness of the preaching **to save those who believe**.

NOTE: This sectional pairing (east and south side) and the next one (west and north side) combine to be part of a larger idea Paul is developing. The layout of this massive campsite in all four directions might look foolish to onlookers, but when viewed from above looks like the sign of the cross! This is the central piece of God's wisdom: **salvation requires belief** that Christ was crucified for our sins.

Num 2:18 "On the **west side** shall be the standard of the camp of Ephraim according to their divisions. The prince of the children of Ephraim shall be Elishama the son of Ammihud. **19** His division, and those who were counted of them, were forty thousand five hundred. **20** "Next to him shall be the tribe of Manasseh. The prince of the children of Manasseh shall be Gamaliel the son of Pedahzur. **21** His division, and those who were counted of them, were thirty-two thousand two hundred. **22** "The tribe of Benjamin: the prince of the children of Benjamin shall be Abidan the son of Gideoni. **23** His army, and those who were counted of them, were thirty-five thousand four hundred. **24** "All who were counted of the camp of Ephraim were one hundred eight thousand one hundred, according to their divisions. They shall set out third.

25 "On the **north side** shall be the standard of the camp of Dan according to their divisions. The prince of the children of Dan shall be Ahiezer the son of Ammishaddai. **26** His division, and those who were counted of them, were sixty-two thousand seven hundred. **27** "Those who encamp next to him shall be the tribe of Asher. The prince of the children of Asher shall be Pagiel the son of Ochran. **28** His division, and those who were counted of them, were forty-one thousand five hundred. **29** "The tribe of Naphtali: the prince of the children of Naphtali shall be Ahira the son of Enan. **30** His division, and those who were counted of them, were fifty-three thousand four hundred. **31** "All who were counted of the camp of Dan were one hundred fifty-seven thousand six hundred. They shall set out last by their standards." **32** These are those who were counted of the children of Israel by their fathers' houses. All who were counted of the camps according to their armies were six hundred three thousand five hundred fifty. **33** But the Levites were not counted among the children of Israel, as Yahweh commanded Moses. **34** Thus the children of Israel did. According to all that Yahweh commanded Moses, so they encamped by their standards, and so they set out, everyone by their families, according to their fathers' houses.

1Cor 1:22 For Jews ask for signs, Greeks seek after wisdom, **23 but we preach Christ crucified**, a stumbling block to Jews and foolishness to Greeks, **24** but to those who are called, both Jews and Greeks, Christ is the **power** of God and the **wisdom** of God; **25** because the **foolishness** of God is wiser than men, and the **weakness** of God is stronger than men.

NOTE: The statement "but we preach Christ crucified" may refer to the entire structure of the campsite which looks like a cross when viewed from above. Continuing from the previous pairing, two more directions are added: west and north. the verses in 1 Corinthians now contrast "wisdom" vs. "foolishness," and "power" vs. "weakness." The upside-down statements such as "foolishness of God is wiser than men" may echo the fact that the campsite structure is symmetrical.

Numbers 3

1 Corinthians 1:26

Num 3:1 Now this is the history of the generations of Aaron and Moses in the day that Yahweh spoke with Moses in Mount Sinai. **2** These are the names of the sons of Aaron: Nadab the firstborn, and Abihu, Eleazar, and Ithamar. **3** These are the names of the sons of Aaron, the priests who were anointed, whom he consecrated to minister in the priest's office. **4 Nadab and Abihu died before Yahweh when they offered strange fire** before Yahweh in the wilderness of Sinai, and they had no children. **Eleazar and Ithamar ministered in the priest's office** in the presence of Aaron their father.

5 Yahweh spoke to Moses, saying, **6** "Bring the tribe of Levi near, and set them before Aaron the priest, that they may minister to him. **7** They shall keep his requirements, and the requirements of the whole congregation before the Tent of Meeting, to do the service of the tabernacle. **8 They shall keep all the furnishings of the Tent of Meeting**, and the obligations of the children of Israel, to do the service of the tabernacle. **9** You shall give the **Levites to Aaron and to his sons. They are wholly given to him on the behalf of the children of Israel**. **10** You shall appoint Aaron and his sons, and they shall **keep their priesthood**, but the stranger who comes near shall be put to death."

1Cor 1:26 For you see your calling, brothers, that **not many are wise according to the flesh, not many mighty, and not many noble**; **27** but God chose the foolish things of the world that he might put to shame those who are wise. God chose the weak things of the world that he might put to shame the things that are strong. **28** God chose the lowly things of the world, and the things that are despised, and the things that don't exist, that he might bring to nothing the things that exist, **29** that no flesh should boast before God. **30 Because of him, you are in Christ Jesus**, who was made to us wisdom from God, and **righteousness and sanctification, and redemption**, **31** that, as it is written, "**He who boasts, let him boast in the Lord.**"

NOTE: 1 Corinthians 1:26-31 seems to echo all of Numbers Ch. 3, not just the first ten verses. Therefore, the final two pairings of Numbers 3 continue to highlight echoes with 1 Corinthians 1:26-31.

Num 3:11 Yahweh spoke to Moses, saying, **12** "Behold, <u>**I have taken the Levites**</u> from among the children of Israel instead of all the firstborn **who open the womb** among the children of Israel; and the Levites shall be mine, **13** for all the firstborn are mine. On the day that I struck down all the firstborn in the land of Egypt, I made holy to me all the firstborn in Israel, both man and animal. They shall be mine. I am Yahweh." **14** Yahweh spoke to Moses in the wilderness of Sinai, saying, **15** "Count the children of Levi by their fathers' houses, by their families. You shall count every male from a month old and upward." **16** Moses counted them according to Yahweh's word, as he was commanded. **17** These were the sons of Levi by their names: Gershon, Kohath, and Merari. **18** These are the names of the sons of Gershon by their families: Libni and Shimei. **19** The sons of Kohath by their families: Amram, Izhar, Hebron, and Uzziel. **20** The sons of Merari by their families: Mahli and Mushi. These are the families of the Levites according to their fathers' houses. **21** <u>**Of Gershon**</u> was the family of the Libnites, and the family of the Shimeites. These are the families of the Gershonites. **22** Those who were counted of them, according to the number of all the males from a month old and upward, even those who were counted of them were seven thousand five hundred. **23** The families of the Gershonites shall encamp behind the tabernacle westward. **24** The prince of the fathers' house of the Gershonites shall be Eliasaph the son of Lael. **25** The duty of the sons of Gershon in the Tent of Meeting shall be the tabernacle, the tent, its covering, the screen for the door of the Tent of Meeting, **26** the hangings of the court, the screen for the door of the court which is by the tabernacle and around the altar, and its cords for all of its service. **27 Of Kohath** was the family of the Amramites, the family of the Izharites, the family of the Hebronites, and the family of the Uzzielites. These are the families of the Kohathites. **28** According to the number of all the males from a month old and upward, there were eight thousand six hundred keeping the requirements of the sanctuary. **29** The families of the sons of Kohath shall encamp on the south side of the tabernacle. **30** The prince of the fathers' house of the families of the Kohathites shall be Elizaphan the son of Uzziel. **31** Their duty shall be the ark, the table, the lamp stand, the altars, the vessels of the sanctuary with which they minister, the screen, and all its service. **32** Eleazar the son of Aaron the priest shall be prince of the princes of the Levites, with the oversight of those who keep the requirements of the sanctuary.

1Cor 1:26 For you see <u>**your calling, brothers**</u>, that not many are wise **according to the flesh**, not many mighty, and not many noble; **27** but <u>**God chose the foolish things of the world**</u> that he might put to shame those who are wise. **God chose the weak things of the world** that he might put to shame the things that are strong.

Num 3:33 Of Merari was the family of the Mahlites and the family of the Mushites. These are the families of Merari. **34** Those who were counted of them, according to the number of all the males from a month old and upward, were six thousand two hundred. **35** The prince of the fathers' house of the families of Merari was Zuriel the son of Abihail. They shall encamp on the north side of the tabernacle. **36** The appointed duty of the sons of Merari shall be the tabernacle's boards, its bars, its pillars, its sockets, all its instruments, all its service, **37** the pillars of the court around it, their sockets, their pins, and their cords. **38** Those who encamp before the tabernacle eastward, in front of the Tent of Meeting toward the sunrise, shall be **Moses, Aaron,** and his sons, keeping the requirements of the sanctuary for the duty of the children of Israel. The outsider who comes near **shall be put to death**. **39** All who were counted of the Levites, whom Moses and Aaron counted at the commandment of Yahweh, by their families, <u>**all the males**</u> from a month old and upward, were twenty-two thousand.

1Cor 1:28 God chose the lowly things of the world, and the <u>**things that are despised**</u>, and the **things that don't exist**, that he might bring to nothing the things that exist, **29** <u>**that no flesh**</u> should boast before God. **30** Because of him, you are in Christ Jesus, who was made to us wisdom from God, and righteousness and sanctification, and redemption, **31** that, as it is written, "He who boasts, let him boast in the Lord."

NOTE: Moses and Aaron were despised by onlookers soon after being chosen by God to lead Israel out of Egypt.

Numbers 3:40 | ## 1 Corinthians 2

Num 3:40 Yahweh said to Moses, "Count all the firstborn males of the **children of Israel from a month old** and upward, and take the number of their names. **41** You shall take the Levites for me—I am Yahweh—instead of all the firstborn among the children of Israel; and the livestock of the Levites instead of all the firstborn among the livestock of the children of Israel." **42** Moses counted, as Yahweh commanded him, all the firstborn among the children of Israel. **43** All the firstborn males according to the number of names from a month old and upward, of those who were counted of them, were twenty-two thousand two hundred seventy-three. **44** Yahweh spoke to Moses, saying, **45** "Take the Levites instead of all the firstborn among the children of Israel, and the livestock of the Levites instead of their livestock; and the Levites shall be mine. **I am Yahweh**. **46** **For the redemption of the two hundred seventy-three of the firstborn of the children of Israel who exceed the number of the Levites**, **47** you shall take five shekels apiece for each one; according to the shekel of the sanctuary you shall take them (the shekel is twenty gerahs); **48** and you shall give the money, with which their remainder is redeemed, to Aaron and to his sons." **49** Moses took the redemption money from those who exceeded the number of those who were redeemed by the Levites; **50** from the firstborn of the children of Israel he took the money, one thousand three hundred sixty-five shekels, according to the shekel of the sanctuary; **51** and Moses gave the redemption money to Aaron and to his sons, according to Yahweh's word, as Yahweh commanded Moses.

1Cor 2:1 When I came to you, brothers, **I didn't come with excellence of speech or of wisdom**, proclaiming to you the testimony of God. **2** For I determined not to know anything among you except **Jesus Christ and him crucified**.

NOTE: The 273 persons from all the other tribes who exceeded the number of the Levites required redemption. In the same way Paul's mission was to share the truth of the redemption possible to worldwide Gentiles made possible through a crucified Messiah.

Numbers 4	1 Cor. 2:3

Num 4:1 Yahweh spoke to Moses and to Aaron, saying, **2** "Count the sons of **Kohath** from among the sons of Levi, by their families, by their fathers' houses, **3** from thirty years old and upward even until fifty years old, **all who enter into the service to do the work in the Tent of Meeting**. **4** "This is the service of the sons of Kohath in the Tent of Meeting, regarding the most holy things.

5 When the camp moves forward, Aaron shall go in with his sons; and they shall take down the **veil of the screen**, cover the **ark of the Testimony** with it, **6** put a covering of sealskin on it, spread a blue cloth over it, and put in its poles. **7** "On the table of show bread, they shall spread a blue cloth, and put on it the dishes, the spoons, the bowls, and the cups with which to pour out; and the continual bread shall be on it. **8 They shall spread on them a scarlet cloth, and cover it with a covering of sealskin, and shall put in its poles**. **9** "They shall take a blue cloth and cover the lamp stand of the light, its lamps, its snuffers, its snuff dishes, and all its oil vessels, with which they minister to it. **10** They shall put it and all its vessels within a covering of sealskin and shall put it on the frame. **11** "<u>On the golden altar they shall spread a blue cloth, and cover it with a covering of sealskin, and shall put in its poles</u>. **12** "They shall take all the vessels of ministry with which they minister in the sanctuary, and put them in a blue cloth, cover them with a covering of sealskin, and shall put them on the frame. **13** "They shall take away the ashes from the altar and spread a purple cloth on it. **14** They shall put on it all its vessels with which they minister about it, the fire pans, the meat hooks, the shovels, and the basins—all the vessels of the altar; and they shall spread on it a covering of sealskin, and put in its poles. **15** "When Aaron and his sons have finished covering the sanctuary and all the furnishings of the sanctuary, as the camp is set forward; after that, the sons of Kohath shall come to carry it; but they shall not **touch the sanctuary, lest they die**. The sons of Kohath shall carry these things in the **Tent of Meeting**.

1Cor 2:3 I was with you in **weakness**, in fear, and in much trembling. **4** My speech and my preaching were **not in persuasive words of human wisdom**, but in demonstration of the **Spirit** and

of **power**, **5** that your faith wouldn't stand in the wisdom of men, but in the power of God. **6** We speak wisdom, however, among those who are full grown, yet a **wisdom not of this world** nor of the rulers of this world who are coming to nothing. **7** But we speak **God's wisdom in a mystery, the wisdom that has been hidden**, which God foreordained before the worlds for our glory, **8** which none of the rulers of this world has known. For had they known it, they wouldn't have **crucified** the **Lord of glory**.

NOTE: Kohath echoes "weakness" in Numbers 3:27 as well. In 1 Corinthians 2 "among those who are full grown" may echo Kohath age requirements in Num. 4:3. The "wisdom not of this world" echoes the unusual instructions to the Levites such as regarding the "scarlet cloth."

Num 4:16 "The duty of Eleazar the son of Aaron the priest shall be the oil for **the light**, the <u>**sweet incense**</u>, the continual meal offering, and the anointing oil, the requirements of all the tabernacle, **and of all that is in it, the sanctuary, and its furnishings**." **17** Yahweh spoke to Moses and to Aaron, saying, **18** "Don't cut off the tribe of the families of the Kohathites from among the Levites; **19** but do this to them, that they may live, and not die, when they approach the most <u>**holy**</u> things: Aaron and his sons shall go in and appoint them each to his **service** and to his **burden**; **20** but they shall not go in to see the sanctuary even for a moment, lest they die."

1Cor 1:9 But as it is written, "**Things which an eye didn't see**, and an ear didn't hear, which didn't enter into the heart of man, these God has prepared for those who love him." **10** But to us, God revealed them <u>**through the Spirit**</u>. For the Spirit searches all things, yes, **the deep things of God**. **11** For who among men knows the things of a man except the spirit of the man which is in him? Even so, no one knows the things of God except God's Spirit. **12** But we received not the spirit of the world, but the Spirit which is from God, that we might know the things that were freely given to us by God. **13** We also speak these things, not in words which man's wisdom teaches but which the <u>**Holy**</u> Spirit teaches, comparing **spiritual things** with **spiritual things**.

NOTE: [Bamidbar ends.] Not only in Numbers/1 Corinthians, but also in Leviticus/Romans are the concepts of aroma and incense are often echoed by Paul in the work of the Holy Spirit. In Hebrew, "Holy Spirit" is *ruach hakodesh* meaning "the holy wind."

Numbers 4:21	1 Cor. 2:14

Num 4:21 Yahweh spoke to Moses, saying, **22** "Take a census of the sons of Gershon also, by their fathers' houses, by their families; **23** you shall count them from thirty years old and upward until fifty years old: all who enter in to wait on the **service**, to do the <u>work</u> in the Tent of Meeting. **24** "This is the <u>service</u> of the families of the **Gershonites**, in serving and in bearing burdens: **25** they shall carry the curtains of the tabernacle and the Tent of Meeting, its covering, the covering of sealskin that is on it, the screen for the door of the Tent of Meeting, **26** the hangings of the court, the screen for the door of the gate of the court which is by the tabernacle and around the altar, their cords, and all the instruments of their <u>service</u>, and whatever shall be done with them. They shall serve in there. **27** At the commandment of Aaron and his sons shall be all the <u>service</u> of the sons of the Gershonites, in all their <u>burden</u> and in all their service; and you shall appoint their duty to them in all their burdens. **28** This is the <u>service</u> of the families of the sons of the Gershonites in the Tent of Meeting. Their duty shall be under the hand of Ithamar the son of Aaron the priest.	**1Cor 2:14** Now the <u>natural man</u> doesn't receive the things of **God's Spirit**, for they are **<u>foolishness</u>** to him; and he can't know them, because they are spiritually discerned. **15** But he who is spiritual discerns all things, and he himself is to be judged by no one. **16** "For who has known the mind of the Lord that he should instruct him?" But we have Christ's mind.

NOTE: [Naso.] See Numbers 3:21 that also connects "Gershonites" to "foolishness." The service of the tent of meeting is indeed seemingly foolish to the natural man.

NOTE: The most common word for service *abodah* in Hebrew, appears six times in the Numbers pairing above. Six is the number of the day man was created. The pairing above also includes a less common word for "**service**," *tsaba* that allows *abodah* to become seven, echoing the spiritual dimension brought in through Shabbat, shown above as "service" in Num. 4:23 echoing "God's Spirit" in 1 Corinthians 2:14.

NOTE: The word for serve, is *abad*, and appears three times, bringing the number to nine, related to the spiritual gifts of the Holy Spirit.

Numbers 4:29	1 Corinthians 3

Num 4:29 "As for the sons of Merari, you shall count them by their families, by their fathers' houses; **30** you shall count them from thirty years old and upward even to fifty years old—everyone who enters on the **service**, to do the work of the Tent of Meeting. **31** This is the duty of their burden, according to all their service in the Tent of Meeting: the tabernacle's **boards, its bars, its pillars, its sockets**, **32** the pillars of the court around it, their sockets, their pins, their cords, with all their instruments, and with all their service. You shall **appoint the instruments of the duty of their burden to them by name**. **33** This is the service of the families of the sons of Merari, according to all their service in the Tent of Meeting, under the hand of Ithamar the son of Aaron the priest."

1Cor 3:1 Brothers, I couldn't speak to you as to **spiritual**, but as to fleshly, as to babies in Christ. **2** I fed you with milk, not with solid food, for you weren't yet ready. Indeed, you aren't ready even now, **3** for you are still fleshly. For insofar as there is **jealousy, strife, and factions among you, aren't you fleshly**, and don't you walk in the ways of men? **4** For when one says, **"I follow Paul," and another, "I follow Apollos," aren't you fleshly**?

5 Who then is Apollos, and who is Paul, but **servants through whom you believed**, and each as the Lord gave to him? **6** I planted. Apollos watered. But God gave the increase. **7** So then neither he who plants is anything, nor he who waters, but God who gives the increase. **8** Now **he who plants and he who waters are the same**, but each will receive his own reward **according to his own labor**.

NOTE: While not bolded, "sons of Merari" in Numbers 4:29 seems to echo "babies in Christ" in 1 Corinthians 3:1. See Num. 3:33 that also connects "Merari" to "lowly things."

NOTE: Similar to the previous pairing, "service" in Num. 4:30 echoes "spiritual" in 1 Cor. 3:1.

Num 4:34 <u>Moses, Aaron, and the princes of the congregation counted the sons of the Kohathites</u> by their families, <u>and by their fathers' houses</u>, **35** from thirty years old and upward even to fifty years old, everyone who entered into the service, for work in the Tent of Meeting. **36** Those who were counted of them by their families were two thousand seven hundred fifty. **37** These are those who were counted of the families of the Kohathites, all who served in the Tent of Meeting, whom Moses and Aaron counted according to the commandment of Yahweh by Moses.

38 Those who were counted of the sons of Gershon, by their families, and **by their fathers' houses**, **39** from thirty years old and upward even to fifty years old—everyone who entered into the service for work in the Tent of Meeting— **40** even those who were counted of them, by their families, <u>by their fathers' houses</u>, were two thousand six hundred thirty. **41** These are those who were counted of the families of the sons of Gershon, all who served in the Tent of Meeting, whom Moses and Aaron counted according to the **commandment of Yahweh**.

42 Those who were counted of the families of the sons of Merari, by their families, <u>by their fathers' houses</u>, **43** from thirty years old and upward even to fifty years old—everyone who entered into the service for work in the Tent of Meeting— **44** even those who were counted of them by their families, were three thousand two hundred. **45** These are those who were counted of the families of the sons of Merari, whom Moses and Aaron counted according to the commandment of Yahweh by Moses.

1Cor 3:9 For we are **God's fellow workers**. You are **God's farming**, <u>God's building</u>.

10 According to the grace of God which was given to me, as a wise master builder **I laid a foundation**, and <u>another builds on it</u>. But let each man be careful how he builds on it. **11** For no one can lay any other foundation than that which has been laid, which is **Jesus Christ**. **12** <u>But if anyone builds on the foundation</u> with gold, silver, costly stones, wood, hay, or straw, **13** each man's work will be revealed. For the Day will declare it, because it is revealed in fire; and the fire itself will test what sort of work each man's work is.

NOTE: The "commandment of Yahweh" is the completely fulfilled in the work of "Jesus Christ" who finished the foundational work of salvation on the cross. Multiple echoes are underlined above connecting "houses" in Numbers to "building" in 1 Corinthians.

Num 4:46 All those who were counted of the Levites whom Moses and Aaron and the princes of Israel counted, by their families and <u>by their fathers' houses</u>, **47** from **thirty years old and upward** even to fifty years old, **everyone who entered in to do the work of service and the work of bearing burdens in the Tent of Meeting**, **48** even those who were counted of them, were **eight thousand five hundred eighty**. **49 According to the commandment of Yahweh** they were counted by Moses, everyone according to his service and according to his burden. **Thus, were they counted by him, as Yahweh commanded** Moses.

1Cor 3:14 If any man's work remains <u>which he built on it</u>, he will receive a reward. **15** If any man's work is burned, he will suffer loss, but he himself will be saved, but as through fire.

16 <u>Don't you know that you are God's temple</u> and that **God's Spirit lives in you**? **17** <u>If anyone destroys God's temple, God will destroy him</u>; for **God's temple is holy, which you are**.

NOTE: Paul is developing the idea that "we are God's temple" by examining the people who serve and word in the Tent of Meeting, and recognizing that these 8,580 Levites were as much a part of the construction of the Tent of Meeting, as the physical elements!

Numbers 5	1 Corinthians 3:18

Num 5:1 Yahweh spoke to Moses, saying, **2** "Command the children of Israel that they put out of the camp every leper, everyone who has a discharge, and whoever is unclean by a corpse. **3** You shall put both male and female outside of the camp so that they don't defile their camp, in the midst of which I dwell." **4 The children of Israel did so, and put them outside of the camp**; as Yahweh spoke to Moses, so the children of Israel did.

5 Yahweh spoke to Moses, saying, **6** "Speak to the children of Israel: 'When a man or woman commits any sin that men commit, so as to trespass against Yahweh, and that soul is guilty, **7 then he shall confess his sin which he has done; and he shall make restitution for his guilt in full, add to it the fifth part of it, and give it to him in respect of whom he has been guilty**. **8** But if the man has no kinsman to whom restitution may be made for the guilt, the restitution for guilt which is made to Yahweh shall be the priest's, in addition to the ram of the atonement, by which atonement shall be made for him. **9 Every heave offering of all the holy things of the children of Israel, which they present to the priest, shall be his.**" **10** Every man's holy things shall be his; whatever any man gives the priest, it shall be his.'"

1Cor 3:18 Let no one deceive himself. If anyone thinks that he is wise among you in this world, **let him become a fool that he may become wise**. **19** For the wisdom of this world is foolishness with God. For it is written, "He has taken the wise in their craftiness." **20** And again, "**The Lord knows the reasoning of the wise, that it is worthless.**" **21** Therefore let no one boast in men. **For all things are yours**, **22** whether Paul, or Apollos, or Cephas, or the world, or life, or death, or things present, or things to come. **All are yours**,

NOTE: The connection between "man or woman" and "world" is simply that the world is full of both genders.

Num 5:11 Yahweh spoke to Moses, saying, **12** "Speak to the children of Israel, and tell them: 'If any man's wife goes astray and is unfaithful to him, **13** and a man lies with her carnally, and it is hidden from the eyes of her husband and this is kept concealed, and she is defiled, there is no witness against her, and she isn't taken in the act; **14** and the spirit of jealousy comes on him, and he is jealous of his wife and she is defiled; or if the spirit of jealousy comes on him, and he is jealous of his wife, and she isn't defiled; **15 then the man shall bring his wife to the priest, and shall bring her offering for her**: one tenth of an ephah of barley meal. He shall pour no oil on it, nor put frankincense on it, for it is a meal offering of jealousy, a meal offering of memorial, bringing iniquity to memory.

16 <u>**The priest shall bring her near and set her before Yahweh**</u>. **17** The priest shall take holy water in an earthen vessel; and the priest shall take some of the dust that is on the floor of the tabernacle and put it into the water. **18** The priest shall set the woman before Yahweh, and let the hair of the woman's head go loose, and put the meal offering of memorial in her hands, which is the meal offering of jealousy. The priest shall have in his hand the water of bitterness that brings a curse. **19** The priest shall cause her to take an oath, and shall tell the woman, "If no man has lain with you, and if you haven't gone aside to uncleanness, being under your husband's authority, be free from this water of bitterness that brings a curse. **20** But if you have gone astray, being under your husband's authority, and if you are defiled, and some man has lain with you besides your husband—" **21** then the priest shall cause the woman to swear with the oath of cursing, and the priest shall tell the woman, "May Yahweh make you a curse and an oath among your people, when Yahweh allows your thigh to fall away, and your body to swell; **22** and this water that brings a curse will go into your bowels, and make your body swell, and your thigh fall away." The woman shall say, "Amen, Amen."

1Cor 3:23 and **you are Christ's**, and <u>**Christ is God's**</u>.

NOTE: Further study of this passage may yield more insights. In the WEB translation we count eight references to the *husband* (husband, man, or him), and nine references *priest*, five references to *Yahweh*, two direct references to spirit, four references to *curse*. It recalls for us Exodus 20:5 "I the Lord your God am a jealous God." The thought occurs to us that Paul, knowing it might take an entire letter to just unpack this portion of Numbers, decided to write a single summary statement and keep moving. He does it again towards the end of his letter (1 Corinthians 14:40).

Num 5:23 "'The priest shall write these curses in a book, and he shall wipe them into the water of bitterness. **24** He shall make the woman drink the water of bitterness that causes the curse; and the water that causes the curse shall enter into her and become bitter. **25** The priest shall take the meal offering of jealousy out of the woman's hand, and shall wave the meal offering before Yahweh, and bring it to the altar. **26** The priest shall take a handful of the meal offering, as its memorial portion, and burn it on the altar, and afterward shall make the woman drink the water. **27** When he has made her drink the water, then it shall happen, if she is defiled and has committed a trespass against her husband, that the water that causes the curse will enter into her and become bitter, and her body will swell, and her thigh will fall away; and the woman will be a curse among her people. **28** If the woman isn't defiled but is clean; then she shall be free, and shall conceive offspring.

29 "'This is the law of jealousy, when a wife, being under her husband, goes astray, and is defiled, **30** or when the spirit of jealousy comes on a man, and he is jealous of his wife; then he shall set the woman before Yahweh, and the priest shall execute on her all this law. **31** The man shall be free from iniquity, and that woman shall bear her iniquity.'"

NOTE: These verses seem to be skipped by Paul. If the layout sizes would have allowed it, these verses would have been included with Numbers 5:11-22 of the previous pairing. The word counts mentioned in the previous pairing do not encompass the verses above. In the WEB translation we count four more mentions of *husband* and four for *priest* two of *Yahweh*, one of *spirit*, and five of *curse*.

Numbers 6

1 Corinthians 4

Num 6:1 Yahweh spoke to Moses, saying, **2** "Speak to the children of Israel, and tell them, 'When either **man or woman** shall make a special vow, **the vow of a Nazirite**, to separate himself to Yahweh, **3** he shall separate himself from wine and strong drink. He shall drink no vinegar of wine, or vinegar of fermented drink, neither shall he drink any juice of grapes, nor eat fresh grapes or dried. **4 All the days of his separation** he shall eat nothing that is made of the grapevine, from the seeds even to the skins.

5 "'All the days of his vow of separation no razor shall come on his head, until the days are fulfilled in which he separates himself to Yahweh. He shall be holy. He shall let the locks of the hair of his head grow long.

6 "'All the days that he separates himself to Yahweh he shall not go near a dead body. **7** He shall not make himself unclean for his father, or for his mother, for his brother, or for his sister, when they die, because his separation to God is on his head. **8 All the days of his separation he is holy to Yahweh**.

9 "'If any man dies very suddenly beside him, and he defiles the head of his separation, then he shall shave his head in the day of his cleansing. On the seventh day he shall shave it. **10 On the eighth day he shall bring two turtledoves or two young pigeons to the priest, to the door of the Tent of Meeting**. **11** The priest shall offer one for a sin offering, and the other for a burnt offering, and make atonement for him, because he sinned by reason of the dead, and shall make his head holy that same day. **12** He shall separate to Yahweh the days of his separation and shall bring a male lamb a year old for a trespass offering; **but the former days shall be void, because his separation was defiled**."

1Cor 4:1 So let a man think of **us** as Christ's servants and **stewards of God's mysteries**. **2** Here, moreover, it is required of stewards **that they be found faithful**. **3** But with me it is a very small thing that I should be judged by you, or by a human court. Yes, I don't even judge myself. **4** For I know nothing against myself. **Yet I am not justified by this, but he who judges me is the Lord**. **5** Therefore **judge nothing before the time, until the Lord comes**, who will both bring to **light the hidden things of darkness** and reveal the counsels of the hearts. Then each man will get his praise from God.

NOTE: One of the mysteries of the Nazarites is the prohibition not only of wine, but of the skins of grapes. Concerning 1 Corinthians 4:4, indeed the only "person" who knows if the Nazarite remained fully separated is the Lord.

Num 6:13 "'This is the law of the Nazirite: when the days of his separation are fulfilled, he shall be brought to the door of the Tent of Meeting, **14** <u>and he shall offer his offering to Yahweh: one male lamb a year old without defect for a burnt offering, one ewe lamb a year old without defect for a sin offering, one ram without defect for peace offerings</u>, **15** a basket of unleavened bread, cakes of fine flour mixed with oil, and unleavened wafers anointed with oil with their meal offering and their drink offerings. **16** The priest shall present them before Yahweh and shall offer his sin offering and his burnt offering. **17** He shall offer the ram for a sacrifice of peace offerings to Yahweh, **with the basket of unleavened bread**. The priest shall offer also its meal offering and its drink offering. **18** The Nazirite shall shave the head of his separation at the door of the Tent of Meeting, take the hair of the head of his separation, and put it on the fire which is under the sacrifice of peace offerings. **19** The priest shall take the boiled shoulder of the ram, one unleavened cake out of the basket, and one unleavened wafer, and **shall put them on the hands of the Nazirite** after he has shaved the head of his separation; **20** and the priest shall wave them for a wave offering before Yahweh. **<u>They are holy for the priest, together with the breast that is waved and the thigh that is offered</u>**. After that the Nazirite may drink wine.

21 "'This is the law of the Nazirite who vows and of his offering to Yahweh for his separation, in addition to that which he is able to afford. According to his vow which he vows, so he must do after the law of his separation.'"

1Cor 4:6 Now these things, brothers, I have in a figure transferred to myself and Apollos for your sakes, <u>that in us you might learn not to think beyond the things which are written</u>, that none of you be **<u>puffed up against one another</u>**. **7** For who makes you different? And **what do you have that you didn't receive**? But **<u>if you did receive it, why do you boast as if you had not received it</u>**?

NOTE: The Nazirite was to give very specific sacrifices as written in the Torah. Paul seems to echo this by saying we should stop trying to outdo each other but focus on doing well what has been given to us to do. Unleavened bread is not puffed up with yeast. The priests received the benefit of the sacrifice given to Yahweh by the Nazarite, and the Nazarite had placed back in his hands part the very sacrifices he was commanded to offer, so that they could be offered as a wave offering. So both parties, Nazarite and priest, are put into a posture of receiving.

Num 6:22 Yahweh spoke to Moses, saying, **23** "**Speak to Aaron and to his sons**, saying, 'This is how you shall **bless the children of Israel**.' You shall tell them,

24 'Yahweh <u>bless you and keep you</u>. **25** Yahweh <u>make his face to shine on you and be gracious to you</u>. **26** Yahweh <u>lift up his face toward you and give you peace</u>.'

27 "So, they shall put my name on the children of **Israel; and I will bless them**."

1**Cor 4:8** You are already filled. You have already become rich. You have come to reign without us. Yes, and I wish that you did reign, that we also might reign with you! **9 For I think that God has displayed us, the apostles, last of all, like men sentenced to death**. For we are made a spectacle to the world, both to angels and men. **10 <u>We are fools for Christ's sake, but you are wise in Christ. We are weak, but you are strong. You have honor, but we have dishonor</u>**. **11** Even to this present hour we hunger, thirst, are naked, are beaten, and have no certain dwelling place. **12** We toil, working with our own hands. <u>When people curse us, we bless</u>. Being <u>persecuted, we endure</u>. **13** Being <u>defamed, we entreat</u>. We are made as the **filth of the world, the dirt wiped off by all, even until now**.

NOTE: Paul is revealing the price of the blessing. The priests, and by implication Christ in his priestly role, had to endure much from the world before He could stand in the positional priestly authority to bless so magnificently. Paul is stating that the price of the benefit that the apostle brings is to be last rather than first, fools for Christ, weak, dishonored, etc. The only usage of the word "bless" in the first half of the book of Numbers is in this chapter. The first and only usage of the word "bless" by Paul in the first half of 1 Corinthians is in this pairing in verse 12.

NOTE: The contrast between "filth of the world…even until now" and "Israel; and I will bless them" is still present even until now. While the modern-day nation of Israel is clearly "blessed by God" it pays a heavy price for that blessing, being considered by many people including many leaders of modern-day nation states to be "the filth of the world."

Numbers 7	1 Corinthians 4:14

Num 7:1 On the day that Moses had finished setting up the tabernacle and had anointed it and sanctified it with all its furniture, and the altar with all its vessels, and had anointed and sanctified them; **2** the princes of Israel, the heads of their fathers' houses, gave offerings. These were the princes of the tribes. These are they who were over those who were counted; **3** and they brought their offering before Yahweh, six covered wagons and twelve oxen; a wagon for every two of the princes, and for each one an ox. They presented them before the tabernacle. **4 Yahweh spoke to Moses, saying, 5 "Accept these from them**, that they may be used in doing the service of the Tent of Meeting; and you shall give them to the Levites, to every man according to his service." **6** Moses took the wagons and the oxen, and gave them to the Levites. **7** He gave two wagons and four oxen to the sons of Gershon, according to their service. **8** He gave four wagons and eight oxen to the sons of Merari, according to their service, **under the direction of Ithamar** the son of Aaron the priest. **9** But to the sons of Kohath he gave none, because the service of the sanctuary belonged to them; they carried it on their shoulders.

10 The princes gave offerings for the dedication of the altar in the day that it was anointed. The princes gave their offerings before the altar. **11** Yahweh said to Moses, "They shall offer their offering, each prince on his day, for the dedication of the altar."

12 He who offered his offering the first day was Nahshon the **son of Amminadab**, of the tribe of Judah, **13** and his offering was: one silver platter, the weight of which was one hundred thirty shekels, one silver bowl of seventy shekels, according to the shekel of the sanctuary, both of them full of fine flour mixed with oil for a meal offering; **14** one golden ladle of ten shekels, full of incense; **15** one young bull, one ram, one male lamb a year old, for a burnt offering; **16** one male goat for a sin offering; **17** and for the sacrifice of peace offerings, two head of cattle, five rams, five male goats, and five male lambs a year old. This was the offering of Nahshon the **son of Amminadab**.

1Cor 4:14 I don't write these things to shame you, but to admonish you **as my beloved children**. **15** For though you have ten thousand **tutors** in Christ, you don't have many **fathers**. For in Christ Jesus, I became your **father** through the Good News.

NOTE: The princes of the tribes were in a sense, children of Moses, and with the encouragement of Yahweh Moses helped distribute to the Levites the gifts that the princes desired to give.

Num 7:18 On the second day Nethanel the son of Zuar, prince of Issachar, gave his offering. 19 He offered for his offering: one silver platter, the weight of which was one hundred thirty shekels, one silver bowl of seventy shekels, according to the shekel of the sanctuary, both of them full of fine flour mixed with oil for a meal offering; 20 one golden ladle of ten shekels, full of incense; 21 one young bull, one ram, one male lamb a year old, for a burnt offering; 22 one male goat for a sin offering; 23 and for the sacrifice of peace offerings, two head of cattle, five rams, five male goats, five male lambs a year old. This was the offering of Nethanel the son of Zuar.

24 On the third day Eliab the son of Helon, prince of the **children** of Zebulun, 25 gave his offering: one silver platter, the weight of which was a hundred and thirty shekels, one silver bowl of seventy shekels, according to the shekel of the sanctuary, both of them full of fine flour mixed with oil for a meal offering; 26 one golden ladle of ten shekels, full of incense; 27 one young bull, one ram, **one male lamb a year old**, for a burnt offering; 28 one male goat for a sin offering; 29 and for the sacrifice of peace offerings, two head of cattle, five rams, five male goats, five male lambs a year old.

This was the offering of Eliab the son of Helon.

4:16 I beg you, therefore, **be imitators of me**. 17 Because of this I have sent Timothy to you, who is my beloved and faithful **child** in the Lord, who will remind you of my **ways which are in Christ**, even as I teach everywhere in every assembly. 18 Now **some are puffed up**, as though I were not coming to you.

NOTE: Paul's phrase "be imitators of me" seems to derive from the structure of Numbers Ch. 7 which is one of the most precisely repetitive passages in the Bible. The echo is proposed appropriately on the second day, which is the first "imitated" section of the chapter.

NOTE: Paul's use of "Some are puffed up" is proposed to be echoed on the third day, the tribe of Zebulun, because the tribe's name means "exalted."

Num 7:30 On the fourth day Elizur the son of Shedeur, prince of the children of Reuben, **31** gave his offering: one silver platter, the weight of which was one hundred thirty shekels, one silver bowl of seventy shekels, according to the shekel of the sanctuary, both of them full of fine flour mixed with oil for a meal offering; **32** one golden ladle of ten shekels, full of incense; **33** one young bull, one ram, one male lamb a year old, for a burnt offering; **34** one male goat for a sin offering; **35** and for the sacrifice of peace offerings, two head of cattle, five rams, five male goats, five male lambs a year old. This was the offering of Elizur the son of Shedeur.

36 On the fifth day Shelumiel the son of Zurishaddai, prince of the children of Simeon, **37** gave his offering: one silver platter, the weight of which was one hundred thirty shekels, one silver bowl of seventy shekels, according to the shekel of the sanctuary, both of them full of fine flour mixed with oil for a meal offering; **38** one golden ladle of ten shekels, full of incense; **39** one young bull, one ram, one male lamb a year old, for a burnt offering; **40** one male goat for a sin offering; **41** and for the sacrifice of peace offerings, two head of cattle, five rams, five male goats, five male lambs a year old: this was the offering of Shelumiel the son of Zurishaddai.

42 On the sixth day, Eliasaph the son of Deuel, prince of the children of Gad, **43** gave his offering: one silver platter, the weight of which was one hundred thirty shekels, one silver bowl of seventy shekels, according to the shekel of the sanctuary, both of them full of fine flour mixed with oil for a meal offering; **44** one golden ladle of ten shekels, full of incense; **45** one young bull, one ram, one male lamb a year old, for a burnt offering; **46** one male goat for a sin offering; **47** and for the sacrifice of peace offerings, two head of cattle, five rams, five male goats, five male lambs a year old. This was the offering of Eliasaph the son of Deuel.

48 On the seventh day Elishama the son of Ammihud, prince of the children of Ephraim, **49** gave his offering: one silver platter, the weight of which was one hundred thirty shekels, one silver bowl of seventy shekels, according to the shekel of the sanctuary, both of them full of fine flour mixed with oil for a meal offering; **50** one golden ladle of ten shekels, full of incense; **51** one young bull, one ram, one male lamb a year old, for a burnt offering; **52** one male goat for a sin offering; **53** and for the sacrifice of peace offerings, two head of cattle, five rams, five male goats, five male lambs a year old. This was the offering of Elishama the son of Ammihud.

NOTE: Having made his desired points in the first three days, Paul appears to skip these verses.

Num 7:54 On the eighth day Gamaliel the son of Pedahzur, prince of the children of Manasseh, **55** gave his offering: one silver platter, the weight of which was one hundred thirty shekels, one silver bowl of seventy shekels, according to the shekel of the sanctuary, both of them full of fine flour mixed with oil for a meal offering; **56** one golden ladle of ten shekels, full of incense; **57** one young bull, one ram, one male lamb a year old, for a burnt offering; **58** one male goat for a sin offering; **59** and for the sacrifice of peace offerings, two head of cattle, five rams, five male goats, five male lambs a year old. This was the offering of Gamaliel the son of Pedahzur.

60 On the ninth day Abidan the son of Gideoni, prince of the children of Benjamin, **61** gave his offering: one silver platter, the weight of which was one hundred thirty shekels, one silver bowl of seventy shekels, according to the shekel of the sanctuary, both of them full of fine flour mixed with oil for a meal offering; **62** one golden ladle of ten shekels, full of incense; **63** one young bull, one ram, one male lamb a year old, for a burnt offering; **64** one male goat for a sin offering; **65** and for the sacrifice of peace offerings, two head of cattle, five rams, five male goats, five male lambs a year old. This was the offering of Abidan the son of Gideoni.

66 On the tenth day Ahiezer the son of Ammishaddai, prince of the children of Dan, **67** gave his offering: one silver platter, the weight of which was one hundred thirty shekels, one silver bowl of seventy shekels, according to the shekel of the sanctuary, both of them full of fine flour mixed with oil for a meal offering; **68** one golden ladle of ten shekels, full of incense; **69** one young bull, one ram, one male lamb a year old, for a burnt offering; **70** one male goat for a sin offering; **71** and for the sacrifice of peace offerings, two head of cattle, five rams, five male goats, five male lambs a year old. This was the offering of Ahiezer the son of Ammishaddai.

72 On the eleventh day Pagiel the son of Ochran, prince of the children of Asher, **73** gave his offering: one silver platter, the weight of which was one hundred thirty shekels, one silver bowl of seventy shekels, according to the shekel of the sanctuary, both of them full of fine flour mixed with oil for a meal offering; **74** one golden ladle of ten shekels, full of incense; **75** one young bull, one ram, one male lamb a year old, for a burnt offering; **76** one male goat for a sin offering; **77** and for the sacrifice of peace offerings, two head of cattle, five rams, five male goats, five male lambs a year old. This was the offering of Pagiel the son of Ochran.

NOTE: Having made his desired points in the first three days, Paul appears to skip these verses.

Num 7:78 On the twelfth day Ahira the son of Enan, prince of the children of Naphtali, **79** gave his offering: one silver platter, the weight of which was one hundred thirty shekels, one silver bowl of seventy shekels, according to the shekel of the sanctuary, both of them full of fine flour mixed with oil for a meal offering; **80** one golden ladle of ten shekels, full of incense; **81** one young bull, one ram, one male lamb a year old, for a burnt offering; **82** one male goat for a sin offering; **83** and for the sacrifice of peace offerings, two head of cattle, five rams, five male goats, five male lambs a year old. This was the offering of Ahira the son of Enan.

84 This was the dedication offering of the altar, on the day when it was anointed, by the princes of Israel: twelve silver platters, twelve silver bowls, twelve golden ladles; **85** each silver platter weighing one hundred thirty shekels, and each bowl seventy; all the silver of the vessels two thousand four hundred shekels, according to the shekel of the sanctuary; **86** the twelve golden ladles, full of incense, weighing ten shekels apiece, according to the shekel of the sanctuary; all the gold of the ladles weighed one hundred twenty shekels; **87** all the cattle for the burnt offering twelve bulls, the rams twelve, the male lambs a year old twelve, and their meal offering; and twelve male goats for a sin offering; **88** and all the cattle for the sacrifice of peace offerings: twenty-four bulls, sixty rams, sixty male goats, sixty male lambs a year old. This was the dedication offering of the altar, after it was anointed.

89 When Moses went into the Tent of Meeting to speak with Yahweh, he heard his voice speaking to him from above the mercy seat that was on the ark of the Testimony, from between the two cherubim; and he spoke to him.

NOTE: [Naso ends.] Having made his desired points in the first three days, Paul appears to skip these verses.

Numbers 8

1 Corinthians 4:19

Num 8:1 Yahweh spoke to Moses, saying, **2** "**Speak** to Aaron, and tell him, 'When you **light the lamps**, the seven lamps shall give light in front of the lamp stand.'" **3** Aaron did so. He lit its lamps to light the area in front of the lamp stand, as Yahweh **commanded** Moses. **4** This was the **work of the lamp stand**, beaten work of gold. From its base to its flowers, it was **beaten work**. He made the lamp stand according to the pattern which Yahweh had shown Moses.

1Cor 4:19 But I will come to you shortly, if the Lord is willing. And I will know, not **the word** of those who are puffed up, but the **power**. **20** For God's Kingdom is not in **word**, but in **power**. **21** What do you want? Shall I come to you with a **rod**, or in love and a spirit of gentleness?

NOTE: [Behaalotecha.] The olive oil used in the lamps was indeed a power source. A "rod" is something that is used to "beat" something or someone.

Numbers 8:6

1 Corinthians 5

Num 8:5 Yahweh spoke to Moses, saying, **6** "Take the Levites from among the children of Israel, **and cleanse them**. **7** You shall do this to them to cleanse them: sprinkle the water of cleansing on them, let them shave their whole bodies with a razor, let them wash their clothes, and cleanse themselves. **8** Then let them take a young bull, and its meal offering, fine flour mixed with oil; and another young bull you shall take for a **sin offering**. **9** You shall present the Levites before the Tent of Meeting. You shall assemble the whole congregation of the children of Israel. **10** You shall present the Levites before Yahweh. The children of Israel shall lay their hands on the Levites, **11** and Aaron shall offer the Levites before Yahweh for a **wave offering** on the behalf of the children of Israel, that they may be there to do the service of Yahweh. **12** The Levites shall lay their hands on the heads of the bulls, and you shall offer the **one for a sin offering** and the other for a **burnt offering to Yahweh, to make atonement for the Levites**. **13** You shall set the Levites before Aaron and before his sons and offer them as a **wave offering** to Yahweh.

1Cor 5:1 It is actually reported that there is **sexual immorality among you**, and such sexual **immorality as is not even named** among the Gentiles, that one has his father's wife. **2** You are **arrogant**, and didn't mourn instead, that **he who had done this deed** might be **removed from among you**. **3** For I most certainly, as being absent in body but **present in spirit**, have already, as though I were present, judged him who has done this thing.

NOTE: The wave offering is essentially an offering in the air, echoing the holy wind, or *spirit*.

Num 8:14 Thus you shall separate the Levites from among the children of Israel, and the Levites shall be mine. **15** "After that, the Levites shall go in to do the service of the Tent of Meeting. You shall cleanse them and offer them as a **wave offering**. **16** For they are wholly given to me from among the children of Israel; instead of all who open the womb, even the firstborn of all the children of Israel, I have taken them to me. **17** For all the firstborn among the children of Israel are mine, both man and animal. **On the day that I struck all the firstborn in the land of Egypt**, I sanctified them for myself. **18** I have taken the Levites instead of all the firstborn among the children of Israel. **19** **I have given the Levites as a gift to Aaron** and to his sons from among the children of Israel, to do the service of the children of Israel in the Tent of Meeting, and to make atonement for the children of Israel, so that there be no **plague** among the children of Israel when the children of Israel come near to the sanctuary."

20 Moses, and Aaron, and all the congregation of the children of Israel did so to the Levites. According to all that Yahweh commanded Moses concerning the Levites, so the children of Israel did to them. **21** The Levites purified themselves from sin, and they washed their clothes; and Aaron offered them for a **wave offering** before Yahweh and Aaron made **atonement** for them to cleanse them. **22** After that, the Levites went in to do their service in the Tent of Meeting before Aaron and before his sons: as Yahweh had commanded Moses concerning the Levites, so they did to them.

23 Yahweh spoke to Moses, saying, **24** "This is what pertains to the Levites: from twenty-five years old and upward they shall go in to wait on the service in the work of the Tent of Meeting; **25** and from the age of fifty years they shall retire from the duty of the service, **and shall serve no more**, **26** **but shall assist their brothers in the Tent of Meeting**, to perform the duty, but shall perform no service. You shall do thus to the Levites concerning their duties."

1Cor 5:4 In the name of our Lord Jesus Christ, when you are gathered together with **my spirit** with the **power of our Lord Jesus** Christ, **5** you are to **deliver such a one to Satan** for the **destruction of the flesh**, that the **spirit** may be **saved** in the **day of the Lord Jesus**.

NOTE: Once again, the wave offering is echoed by the word *spirit*.

NOTE: The "*day* of the Lord Jesus" seems to echo the *day* when a Levite turns fifty years old and serves no more, but moves into a new phase of his life, a new role. In this sense the "day" is not just a single day in time, but a transitional day that marks the turning point from one phase in time, to another phase in time.

Numbers 9 | 1 Corinthians 5:6

Num 9:1 Yahweh spoke to Moses in the wilderness of Sinai, in the first month of the second year after they had come out of the land of Egypt, saying, **2** "Let the children of Israel <u>keep the Passover</u> in its appointed season. **3** On the fourteenth day of this month, at evening, you shall keep it in its appointed season. You shall keep it according to all its statutes and according to all its ordinances." **4** Moses told the children of Israel that they should <u>keep the Passover</u>.

5 <u>**They kept the Passover in the first month, on the fourteenth day of the month at evening, in the wilderness of Sinai. According to all that Yahweh commanded Moses, so the children of Israel did**</u>. **6** There were certain men who were unclean because of the dead body of a man, so that they could not <u>keep the Passover</u> on that day, and they came before Moses and Aaron on that day. **7** Those men said to him, "We are unclean because of the dead body of a man. Why are we kept back, that we may not offer the offering of Yahweh in its appointed season among the children of Israel?" **8** Moses answered them, "Wait, that I may hear what Yahweh will command concerning you."

9 Yahweh spoke to Moses, saying, **10** "Say to the children of Israel, 'If any man of you or of your generations is unclean by reason of a dead body, or is on a journey far away, he shall still <u>keep the Passover</u> to Yahweh. **11** In the second month, on the fourteenth day at evening they shall keep it; they shall eat it with unleavened bread and bitter herbs. **12** They shall leave none of it until the morning, nor break a bone of it. According to all the statute of the Passover they shall keep it. **13** But the man who is clean, and is not on a journey, and fails to <u>keep the Passover</u>, that soul shall be cut off from his people. Because he didn't offer the offering of Yahweh in its appointed season, that man shall bear his sin. **14** If a foreigner lives among you and desires to <u>keep the Passover</u> to Yahweh, then he shall do so according to the statute of the Passover, and according to its ordinance. You shall have one statute, both for the foreigner and for him who is born in the land.'"

1Cor 5:6 Your boasting is not good. Don't you know that a little yeast leavens the whole lump?

7 <u>Purge out the old yeast</u>, that you may be a new lump,

<u>even as you are unleavened</u>.

For indeed **Christ, our Passover, has been sacrificed in our place**.

8 Therefore let's <u>keep the feast</u>,

<u>not with old yeast</u>,

neither with <u>the yeast of malice and wickedness</u>,

but with the <u>unleavened bread of sincerity and truth</u>.

NOTE: These passages contain the first mention of Passover in Numbers and the only mention of Passover in 1 Corinthians. Paul gives six different exhortations in 1 Corinthians on how to "keep the Passover" echoing the six mentions of "keep the Passover" in Numbers. Paul's central phrase in 1 Cor. 5:7 "Christ our Passover *has been* sacrificed" echoes the historical statement that the Children of Israel "*kept* the Passover" in Num. 9:5. Notice the double nature of "malice and wickedness" and "sincerity and truth" echoes Numbers 9:14 which is directed to both the "foreigner and the native."

Num 9:15 On the day that the tabernacle was raised up, the **cloud covered** the tabernacle, even the Tent of the Testimony. At evening it was over the tabernacle, as it were the appearance of fire, until morning. **16** So it was continually. The **cloud covered** it, and the appearance of fire by night. **17** Whenever the cloud was taken up from over the Tent, then after that the children of Israel traveled; and in the place where the cloud remained, there the children of Israel encamped. **18** At the commandment of Yahweh, the children of Israel traveled, and at the commandment of Yahweh they encamped. As long as the cloud remained over the tabernacle, **they remained encamped**. **19** When the cloud stayed on the tabernacle many days, then the children of Israel kept Yahweh's command, and didn't travel. **20** Sometimes the cloud was a few days on the tabernacle; then according to the commandment of Yahweh they remained encamped, and according to the commandment of Yahweh they traveled. **21** Sometimes the cloud was from evening until morning; and when the cloud was taken up in the morning, they traveled; or by day and by night, when the cloud was taken up, they traveled. **22** Whether it was two days, or a month, or a year that the cloud stayed on the tabernacle, remaining on it, the children of Israel **remained encamped**, and didn't travel; but when it was taken up, they traveled. **23** At the commandment of Yahweh they encamped, and at the commandment of Yahweh they traveled. They kept Yahweh's command, at the commandment of Yahweh by Moses.

1Cor 5:9 I wrote to you in my letter to have no company with **sexual sinners**;

10 yet not at all meaning with the **sexual sinners** of this world, or with the covetous and extortionists, or with idolaters, for then you would have to leave the world. **11** But as it is, I wrote to you not to **associate with anyone who is called a brother** who is a sexual sinner, or covetous, or an idolater, or a slanderer, or a drunkard, or an extortionist. Don't even **eat with such a person**.

NOTE: This passage in Numbers contains the word cloud eleven times: five times before the echo "they remained encamped" and six times after. Similarly, Paul writes of eleven sins: five times before "called a brother" and six times after. They are: sexual sinners, sexual sinners, covetous, extortionists, idolaters; and sexual sinner, covetous, idolater, slanderer, drunkard, and extortionist.

NOTE: As seen once again in this pairing, Paul's practice of exactly matching the count is common in Paul's writings. Why is Paul so particular is his counting? One of his potential motivations might have simply been *respect for God*. If his divinely inspired outline used a given word a certain number of times, then Paul might have reasoned 'who am I to depart from that?' In fact, we find this exact thought from Paul one chapter earlier in 1 Cor. 4:6 "that in us you might learn not to think beyond the things which are written."

Numbers 10

1 Corinthians 5:12

Num 10:1 Yahweh spoke to Moses, saying, **2** "Make two trumpets of silver. You shall make them of beaten work. You shall use them for **the calling of the congregation and for the journeying of the camps**. **3** When they blow them, all the congregation <u>shall gather themselves to you</u> at the door of the Tent of Meeting. **4** If they blow just one, then the princes, the heads of the thousands of Israel, shall gather themselves to you. **5** When you blow an alarm, the camps that lie on the east side shall go forward. **6** When you blow an alarm the second time, the camps that lie on the south side shall go forward. They shall blow an alarm for their journeys. **7** But when the assembly is to be gathered together, you shall blow, but you shall not sound an alarm. **8** "The sons of Aaron, the priests, shall blow the trumpets. This shall be to you for a statute forever throughout your generations. **9** When you go to war in your land against the adversary who oppresses you, then you shall sound an alarm with the trumpets. Then you will be remembered before Yahweh your God, and **you will be saved from your enemies**. **10** "Also in the day of your gladness, and in your set feasts, and in the beginnings of your months, you shall blow the trumpets over your burnt offerings, and over the sacrifices of your peace offerings; and they shall be to you for a memorial before your God. I am Yahweh your God."

1Cor 5:12 For <u>**what do I have to do with also judging those who are outside**</u>?

Don't you <u>judge those who are within</u>?

13 But **those who are outside, God judges.** "Put away the wicked man from among yourselves."

NOTE: The trumpets were used to call the congregation together. But trumpets were also used in wartime and Paul's point in 1 Corinthians 5:13 is that God is the one who judges outside the congregation.

Numbers 10:11	1 Corinthians 6

Num 10:11 In the second year, in the second month, on the twentieth day of the month, the cloud was taken up from over the tabernacle of the Testimony. **12** The **children of Israel** traveled by their journeys out of the wilderness of Sinai; and the cloud stayed in the wilderness of Paran. **13** They first went forward according to the commandment of Yahweh by Moses. **14** First, the standard of the **camp of the children of Judah went forward according to their armies**. Nahshon the son of Amminadab was over his army. **15** Nethanel the son of Zuar was over the army of the tribe of the children of Issachar. **16** Eliab the son of Helon was over the army of the tribe of the children of Zebulun.

17 The tabernacle was taken down; and the sons of Gershon and the sons of Merari, who bore the tabernacle, went forward. **18** The standard of the camp of Reuben went forward according to their armies. Elizur the son of Shedeur was over his army. **19** Shelumiel the son of Zurishaddai was over the **army of the tribe of the children of Simeon**. **20** Eliasaph the son of Deuel was over the army of the tribe of the children of Gad.

21 The Kohathites set forward, bearing the sanctuary. The others set up the tabernacle before they arrived. **22** The standard of the camp of the children of Ephraim set forward according to their armies. Elishama the son of Ammihud was over his army. **23** Gamaliel the son of Pedahzur was over the army of the tribe of the children of Manasseh. **24** Abidan the son of Gideoni was over the army of the tribe of the children of Benjamin.

25 The standard of the camp of the children of **Dan**, which was the **rear guard** of all the camps, set forward according to their armies. Ahiezer the son of Ammishaddai was over his army. **26** Pagiel the son of Ochran was over the army of the tribe of the children of Asher. **27** Ahira the son of Enan was over the army of the tribe of the children of Naphtali. **28** Thus were the travels of the **children of Israel** according to their armies; and they went forward.

1Cor 6:1 Dare any of you, having a matter against his **neighbor**, go to law before the unrighteous, and not before the saints? **2** Don't you know that the **saints will judge the world**? And if the world is judged by you, are you unworthy to judge the **smallest matters**? **3** Don't you know that we will judge angels? How much more, things that pertain to this life? **4** If then you have to **judge things pertaining to this life**, do you set them to judge who are of no account in the assembly? **5** I say this to **move you to shame**. Isn't there even one wise man among you who would be able to decide between his brothers? **6** But **brother** goes to law with brother, and that before unbelievers!

NOTE: While Paul first echoes "Children of Israel" in the wilderness, with the word "neighbor," in the final echo, in the context of going forward together, he chooses "brother." Simeon is proposed to echo "smallest matters" because it will be the smallest tribe in the Numbers 26 census. The word *Dan* means *judge*. While the "rear guard" is a place of honor – avoiding the loss of any that fall behind – Paul's contention is that the church in Corinth is passive. A passive rear guard would definitely be a shame to the procession.

Num 10:29 Moses said to Hobab, the son of Reuel the Midianite, Moses' father-in-law, "We are journeying to the place of which Yahweh said, 'I will give it to you.' Come with us, and we will treat you well; for Yahweh has spoken good concerning Israel." **30 He said to him, "I will not go; but I will depart to my own land, and to my relatives."** 31 Moses said, **"Don't leave us, please**; because you know how we are to encamp in the wilderness, and you can be our eyes. **32** It shall be, if you go with us—yes, it shall be—that whatever good Yahweh does to us, we will do the same to you."

1Cor 6:7 Therefore **it is already altogether a defect in you that you have lawsuits one with another**. Why not rather be wronged? Why not rather be defrauded? 8 No, but you yourselves do wrong and defraud, and that against your brothers. 9 Or don't you know that the unrighteous will not inherit God's Kingdom? **Don't be deceived**.

Neither the sexually immoral, nor idolaters, nor adulterers, nor male prostitutes, nor homosexuals, **10** nor thieves, nor covetous, nor drunkards, nor slanderers, nor extortionists, will inherit God's Kingdom.

NOTE: The ten sins listed in 1 Cor. 6:9-10 may have been inspired by the Ten Commandments, with an emphasis on sexual sin. Could it be that the reason the Midianites would not join with the Children of Israel was that it would require repentance for sexual sin? Indeed, later in Numbers the Midianites would tempt the Children of Israel with that very thing, bringing a plague upon them.

Num 10:33 They set out from the mountain of Yahweh three days' journey. The ark of Yahweh's covenant went before them **three days' journey, to seek out a resting place for them**. 34 The cloud of Yahweh was over them by day, when they set forward from the camp.

35 When the **ark went forward, Moses said, "Rise up, Yahweh**, and let your enemies be scattered! Let those who hate you flee before you!" **36 When it rested, he said, "Return, Yahweh**, to the ten thousands of the thousands of Israel."

1Cor 6:11 Some of you were such, but you were washed.

You were sanctified.

You were justified in the **name of the Lord Jesus**, and in the **Spirit of our God**.

NOTE: Those who remained were led on a three-day journey echoing sanctification. Notice that Moses spoke the name "Yahweh" out loud in this passage.

Numbers 11	1 Corinthians 6:12

Num 11:1 The people were complaining in the ears of Yahweh. When Yahweh heard it, his anger burned; and Yahweh's fire burned among them and consumed some of the outskirts of the camp. **2** The people cried to Moses; and Moses prayed to Yahweh, and the fire abated. **3** The name of that place was called Taberah, because Yahweh's fire burned among them.

4 The mixed multitude that was among them **lusted exceedingly**; and the children of Israel also wept again, and said, "Who will give us **meat to eat**? **5** We remember the <u>fish, which we ate</u> in Egypt for nothing; the cucumbers, and the melons, and the leeks, and the onions, and the garlic; **6** but now **we have lost our appetite. There is nothing** at all **except this manna** to look at."

7 The manna was like coriander seed, and its appearance like the appearance of bdellium. **8** The people went around, gathered it, and ground it in mills, or beat it in mortars, and boiled it in pots, and made cakes of it. Its taste was like the **taste** of fresh **oil**. **9** When the dew fell on the camp in the night, the manna fell on it.

1Cor 6:12 "All things are lawful for me," but not all things are expedient. "All things are lawful for me," but **I will not be brought under the power of anything**.

13 "**<u>Foods for the belly</u>**, and the <u>belly for foods</u>,"

but God will **bring to nothing both it and them**. But the body is not for sexual immorality, but for the Lord, and the Lord for the body. **14** Now God raised up the Lord, and will also raise us up by his power. **15** Don't you know that your **bodies are members of Christ**? Shall I then take the members of Christ and make them members of a prostitute? May it never be! **16** Or don't you know that he who is joined to a prostitute is one body? **For, "The two", he says, "will become one flesh."** **17** But he who is joined to the Lord is one spirit. **18** Flee sexual immorality! "Every sin that a man does is outside the body," but he who commits sexual immorality sins against his own body. **19** Or don't you know that your body is a temple of the Holy Spirit who is in you, whom you have from God? You are not your own, **20** for you were bought with a price. Therefore, glorify God in your **body** and in your **spirit**, which are God's.

NOTE: To lust exceedingly is to be brought under its power. In 1 Corinthians 6:15, Paul echoes God's prefiguring that the nation of Israel would be joined to God through the eating of the manna/Christ. In 1 Cor. 6:16, Paul notices that the manna was like two things: coriander seed, and bdellium.

Numbers 11:10   1 Corinthians 7

Num 11:10 Moses heard the people weeping throughout their families, every man at the door of his tent; and Yahweh's anger burned greatly; and Moses was displeased. **11** Moses said to Yahweh, "Why have you treated your servant so **badly**? Why haven't I found favor in your sight that you **lay the burden** of all this people on me? **12** Have I conceived all this people? Have I brought them out, that you should tell me, 'Carry them in your bosom, as a nurse carries a nursing infant,' to the land which you swore to their fathers? **13 Where could I get meat to give all these people**? For they weep before me, saying, 'Give us meat, that we may eat.' **14** I am not able to bear all this people alone, because it is too heavy for me. **15 If you treat me this way, please kill me right now**, if I have found favor in your sight; and don't let me see my wretchedness."

16 Yahweh said to Moses, "Gather to me seventy men of the elders of Israel, whom you know to be the elders of the people and officers over them; and bring them to the Tent of Meeting, that they may stand there with you. **17 I will come down and talk with you there**. I will take of the Spirit which is on you and will put it on them; and they shall bear the burden of the people with you, that you don't bear it yourself alone.

1Cor 7:1 Now concerning the things about which you wrote to me: it is good for a man not to touch a woman. **2** But, because of **sexual immoralities**, let each man have his own wife, and let each woman have her own husband. **3** Let the **husband give his wife** the affection owed her, and likewise also the wife her husband. **4 The wife doesn't have authority over her own body**, but the husband does. Likewise, also the **husband doesn't have authority over his own body**, but the wife does.

NOTE: Paul's decision to echo the intimate conversation between God and Moses in the embodiment of husband and wife is profound. As the wife doesn't have authority over her own body, so Moses does not have authority to release the burden (the people) that God gave him to carry. But within that intimate relationship he can speak fully from his heart, and even with honest frustration about what he needs as in Numbers 11:15. God then speaks lovingly in Num. 11:17 and says He will come down and talk to Moses and bring him help.

Num 11:18 "Say to the people, 'Sanctify yourselves in preparation for tomorrow, and you will eat meat; for you have *wept in the ears of Yahweh*, saying, "Who will give us meat to eat? For it was well with us in Egypt." Therefore, Yahweh will give you meat, and *you will eat*. **19** You will not eat just one day, or two days, or five days, or ten days, or twenty days, **20** but a whole month, until it comes out at your nostrils, and it is loathsome to you; because you have rejected Yahweh who is among you, and have wept before him, saying, "Why did we come out of Egypt?"'" **21** Moses said, "The people, among whom I am, are *six hundred thousand men* on foot; and you have said, 'I will give them meat, that they may eat a whole month.' **22** Shall **flocks and herds** be slaughtered for them, to be sufficient for them? Shall all the **fish of the sea** be gathered together for them, to be sufficient for them?" **23** Yahweh said to Moses, "Has Yahweh's hand grown short? Now you will see whether my word will happen to you or not." **24** Moses went out and told the people Yahweh's words; and he gathered seventy men of the elders of the people, and set them around the Tent. **25** Yahweh came down in the cloud, and spoke to him, and took of the Spirit that was on him, and put it on the seventy elders. When the Spirit rested on them, they prophesied, but they did so no more.

1Cor 7:5 Don't deprive one another, unless it is by consent for a season, that you may give yourselves to fasting and *prayer*, and may be together again, that **Satan doesn't tempt you** because of your lack of self-control. **6** But this I say by way of *concession*, not of commandment. **7** Yet I wish that *__all men__* were like me. However, each man has his own gift from God, **one of this kind**, and **another of that kind**. **8** But I say to the unmarried and to widows, it is good for them if they remain even as I am. **9** But if they don't have self-control, let them marry. For it's better to marry than to burn with passion.

NOTE: The echo of "eat meat" and "fasting" is explained by the fact that up until this point, the Children of Israel had *not* eaten meat, and so were in a sense *fasting* from the eating of meat. Paul takes this, and their weeping and echoes to the Corinthians "fasting and prayer." However, since there was not consent in Israel to continue that fast, it ended, so that they would not fall into sin.

Num 11:26 But two men **remained in the camp**. The name of one was Eldad, and the name of the other Medad; and the Spirit rested on them. They were of those who were written but had not **gone out** to the Tent; and they prophesied in the camp. **27** A young man ran, and told Moses, and said, "Eldad and Medad are prophesying in the camp!" **28** Joshua the son of Nun, the servant of Moses, one of his chosen men, answered, "My lord Moses, forbid them!" **29** Moses said to him, "Are you jealous for my sake? I wish that all Yahweh's people were prophets, that Yahweh would **put his Spirit on them**!" **30** Moses **went into** the camp, he and the elders of Israel.

1Cor 7:10 But to the married I command—not I, but the Lord—that the wife **not leave** her husband **11** (but if she **departs**, let her remain unmarried, or else **be reconciled** to her husband), and that the husband **not leave** his wife.

NOTE: The two men who *remained* in the camp model the idea of the wife who does *not leave* her husband. These men model "Yahweh's people," echoing the wife as the bride of Christ.

Num 11:31 A wind from Yahweh went out and brought quails from the sea, **and let them fall by the camp, about a day's journey** on this side, and a day's journey on the other side, around the camp, and about two cubits above the surface of the earth. **32** The people rose up all that day, and all of that night, and all the next day, and gathered the quails. He who gathered least gathered ten homers; and they spread them all out for themselves **around the camp**. **33** While the meat was still between their teeth, before it was chewed, Yahweh's anger burned against the people, and Yahweh struck the people with a very great **plague**. **34** The name of that place was called Kibroth Hattaavah, because **there they buried the people who lusted**. **35** From Kibroth Hattaavah the people **traveled to Hazeroth; and they stayed at Hazeroth**.

1Cor 7:12 But to the rest I—not the Lord—say, if any brother has an unbelieving wife, and she is content to live with him, let him not leave her. **13** The woman who has an unbelieving husband, and he is content to live with her, let her not leave her husband.

NOTE: The echo here from Paul is thematic of the passage: the camp and the quails outside of the camp. It is a split situation: they desire to eat meat, but the meat is outside of the camp. Those who were content with manna stayed in the camp, while the others went outside of the camp a day's journey, but apparently returned in the evening. God was not happy with the situation -- He struck them with a plague -- but did not forcibly separate the two groups from each other permanently. Ultimately, when the full month was over, and the supply of quails had ended, all the people came back together and then travelled to Hazeroth *together*, as implied by its name: *settlement*.

Numbers 12	1 Corinthians 7:14
Num 12:1 Miriam and Aaron spoke against Moses because of the **Cushite woman whom he had married**; for he had married a Cushite woman. **2** They said, "Has Yahweh indeed spoken only with **Moses**? Hasn't he spoken also with **us**?" And Yahweh heard it. **3** Now the man **Moses** was very humble, more than all the men who were on the surface of the earth. **4** Yahweh spoke suddenly to **Moses, to Aaron, and to Miriam**, "You three **come out** to the door of the Tent of Meeting!" The three came out.	**1Cor 7:14** For the unbelieving husband is sanctified in the wife, and the **unbelieving wife** is sanctified in the husband. Otherwise, your children would be unclean, but now they are holy. **15** <u>Yet if the unbelieving departs, let there be separation</u>. The **brother or the sister** is not under bondage in such cases, but God has called us in peace. **16** For how do you know, wife, whether you will save your **husband**? Or how do you know, husband, whether you will save your wife? **17** Only, as the Lord has distributed to each man, as <u>**God has called each**</u>, so let him **walk**. So, I ordain in all the assemblies.

NOTE: Paul echoes the situation in which Moses found himself, to be echoed in a believer with an unbelieving wife. While Paul's use of "brother or the sister" is meant in the sense of the body of Christ, this passage, which echoes the complaint of Aaron and Miriam, Moses' brother and sister, it is the first use of the word "sister" by Paul and one of only two mentions of that word in the letter (1 Cor. 9:5).

Num 12:5 The Lord came down in a pillar of cloud, and stood at the door of the Tent of Meeting, and **called Aaron** and Miriam and; they both came forward.

6 He said, "**Now hear my words**. If there is a prophet among you are, I, Yahweh, will make myself known to him in a vision. I will speak with him in a dream. **7 My servant Moses** is not so. He is faithful in all my house. **8** With him, I speak mouth to mouth, even plainly, and not plainly but clearly; in riddles; and he sees the form of God. **Why then were you not afraid** to speak against my servant, against Moses?"

1Cor 7:18 Was anyone **called having been circumcised**? Let him not become uncircumcised. Has anyone been called in uncircumcision? Let him not be circumcised. **19** Circumcision is nothing, and uncircumcision is nothing. But what matters is keeping **God's commandments**. **20** Let each man stay in that calling in which he was called. **21** Were you called being a bondservant? Don't care about it. But if you are able to become free, use it rather. **22** For he who was called in the Lord being a bondservant is the Lord's freed person. **Likewise, he who was called being free is Christ's bondservant**. **23** You were bought with a price. Don't become bondservants of men. **24** Brothers, let each one, in whatever way he was called, remain in that way with God. **25** **Now concerning virgins, I have no commandment from the Lord, but I give my judgment** as one who has obtained mercy from the Lord to be trustworthy. **26** Therefore I think that because of the present distress, it is good for a man to remain as he is.

NOTE: Numbers 12:7 is the first time in this book that God refers to Moses as His servant. 1 Corinthians 7:22 is the first time in 1 Corinthians that Paul mentions being a slave/bondservant. Paul's shift to discussing virgins in v25 may echo God's address to Miriam in Numbers 12:8, who does not command her, but instead questions her judgment.

Num 12:9 The anger of the Lord burned against them; and they he also departed. **10** The cloud went from over the Tent, and behold, **Miriam was leprous**, as white as snow. **Aaron** looked at Miriam, and behold, and behold she was leprous. **11** Aaron said to Moses, "**Oh, my lord, please don't count this sin against us**, in which we have done foolishly, and in which we have sinned. **12** Let her not, I pray, **be as one dead**, of whom the flesh is half consumed when he comes out of his mother's womb."

1Cor 7:27 Are you bound to a wife? Don't seek to be freed. Are you free from a wife? Don't seek a wife. **28** But if you marry, you have not sinned. If a virgin marries, she has not sinned. **Yet such will have oppression in the flesh**, and I want to spare you. **29** But I say this, **brothers**: the time is short. From now on, that those who have wives may be as though they had none; **30 and those who weep**, as though they didn't weep; and those who rejoice, as though they didn't rejoice; and those who buy, as though they didn't possess; **31** and those who use the world, as not using it to the fullest. For the **mode of this world passes away**.

Num 12:13 Moses **cried** to the Lord God, saying, "**Heal her, God, I beg you**!" **14** The Lord said to Moses, "If her father had but spit in her *face*, wouldn't she be **ashamed** seven days? Let her be **shut up** outside of the camp *seven days*, and after that she shall be brought in again." **15** Miriam was ***shut up outside of the tent*** of meeting for seven days, and days the people didn't travel until Miriam the seventh day of her cleansing; and she was brought in again.

16 Afterward the people **traveled from Hazeroth** and encamped in the wilderness of **Paran**.

1Cor 7:32 But I desire to have you to be free from cares. He who is unmarried is concerned for the things of the Lord, how he may please the Lord; **33** but he who is married is **concerned** about the things of the world, **how he may please** his wife. **34** There is also a difference between a wife and a virgin. The unmarried woman cares about the things of the Lord, that she may be holy both in ***body*** and in **spirit**. But she who is married cares about the things of the world—how she may please her husband. **35** This I say for your own benefit, not that I may **ensnare** you, but for that which is *appropriate*, and that you may attend to the Lord without distraction. **36** But if any man thinks that he is behaving inappropriately toward his virgin, if she is past the flower of her age, and if need so requires, let him do what he desires. He doesn't sin. Let them marry. **37** But he who stands steadfast in his heart, having no urgency, but has power over his own will, and has determined in his own heart to keep his own virgin, does well. **38** So then both he who gives his own virgin in marriage does well, and he who doesn't give her in marriage does better. **39** A wife is ***bound by law*** for as long as her husband lives; but if the husband is dead, she is free to be married to whomever she desires, only in the Lord. **40** But she is **happier if she stays** as she is, in my judgment, and I think that I also have **God's Spirit**.

NOTE: [Behaalotecha ends.] Paran is first mentioned in Genesis 21:21 where Ishmael took a wife. Paran means "a place of caverns." David "rose up" and mourned Samuel's death in Paran (1 Samuel 25:1). The Lord "rose up" an adversary to Solomon from Edom, Hadad, (1 Kings 11:14) who with his people "rose up" from Midian and came to Paran (1 Ki. 11:18), all hinting but not overly stating that God's Spirit was the director. In the same way Paul states "*I think that I also have* God's Spirit."

Numbers 13

1 Corinthians 8

Num 13:1 Yahweh spoke to Moses, saying, **2** "Send men, that they may spy out the land of **Canaan**, which I give to the children of Israel. Of every tribe of their fathers, you shall send a man, **every one a prince among them**." **3** Moses sent them from the wilderness of Paran according to the commandment of Yahweh. All of them were **men who were heads** of the children of Israel. **4** These were their names: Of the tribe of Reuben, Shammua the son of Zaccur. **5** Of the tribe of Simeon, Shaphat the son of Hori. **6** Of the tribe of Judah, Caleb the son of Jephunneh. **7** Of the tribe of Issachar, Igal the son of Joseph. **8** Of the tribe of Ephraim, Hoshea the son of Nun. **9** Of the tribe of Benjamin, Palti the son of Raphu. **10** Of the tribe of Zebulun, Gaddiel the son of Sodi. **11** Of the tribe of Joseph, of the tribe of Manasseh, Gaddi the son of Susi. **12** Of the tribe of Dan, Ammiel the son of Gemalli. **13** Of the tribe of Asher, Sethur the son of Michael. **14** Of the tribe of Naphtali, Nahbi the son of Vophsi. **15** Of the tribe of Gad, Geuel the son of Machi. **16** These are the names of the men who Moses sent to spy out the land. Moses called Hoshea the son of Nun Joshua.

17 Moses sent them to spy out the land of Canaan, and said to them, "Go up this way by the South, and go up into the hill country. **18 See the land, what it is**; and the people who dwell therein, whether they are strong or weak, whether they are few or many; **19** and what the land is that they dwell in, whether it is good or bad; and what cities they are that they dwell in, whether in camps, or in strongholds; **20** and what the land is, whether it is fertile or poor, whether there is wood therein, or not. **Be courageous and bring some of the fruit of the land**." Now the time was the time of the first-ripe grapes.

21 So they went up and spied out the land from the wilderness of Zin to Rehob, to the entrance of Hamath. **22** They went up by the South and came to Hebron; and Ahiman, Sheshai, and Talmai, the children of Anak, were there. (Now Hebron was built seven years before Zoan in Egypt.)

1Cor 8:1 Now concerning **things sacrificed to idols**: We know that **we all have knowledge**. **Knowledge puffs up**, but love builds up. **2** But **if anyone thinks that he knows** anything, **he doesn't yet know as he ought to know**.

NOTE: [Shelach.] The work of the spying out the land was all about gathering knowledge. The problem with knowledge is those who have it often believe that by it they have discerned God's will. We don't typically think of the ten spies as being puffed up. But Paul does not stop there, he rightly claims that none of the twelve truly knew "as they ought to know."

Num 13:23 They came to the valley of Eshcol and <u>cut down from there a branch with one cluster of grapes</u>, and they bore it on a staff between two. They also brought some of the pomegranates and figs. **24** That place was called the valley of Eshcol, because of the cluster which the children of Israel cut down from there.

25 They returned from spying out the land at the end of forty days. **26** They went and came to Moses, to Aaron, and to all the congregation of the children of Israel, to the wilderness of Paran, to Kadesh; and brought back word to them and to all the congregation and showed them the fruit of the land. **27** They told him, and said, "We came to the land where you sent us. **Surely it flows with milk and honey, and this is its fruit**. **28** However, the people who dwell in the land are strong, and the cities are fortified and very large. Moreover, **we saw the children of Anak there! 29** Amalek dwells in the land of the South. The Hittite, the Jebusite, and the Amorite dwell in the hill country. The Canaanite dwells by the sea, and along the side of the Jordan."

30 Caleb stilled the people before Moses, and said, "Let's go up at once, <u>and possess it;</u> for **we are well able to overcome it!**" **31** But the men who went up with him said, "*<u>We aren't able to go up against the people; for they are stronger than we</u>*." **32** They brought up an **evil** report of the land which they had spied out to the children of Israel, saying, "The land, through which we have gone to spy it out, is a land that <u>eats</u> up its inhabitants; and all the people who we saw in it are men of great stature. **33** There we saw the Nephilim, the sons of Anak, who come from the Nephilim. We were in our own sight as grasshoppers, and so we were in their sight."

1Cor 8:3 But <u>if anyone loves God, the same is known by him</u>. **4** Therefore concerning the **eating of things sacrificed to idols**, we know that no idol is anything in the world, and that there is no other God but one. **5** For though there are **things that are called "gods", whether in the heavens or on earth**—as there are many "gods" and many "lords"— **6** yet to us there is one God, the Father, <u>of whom are all things</u>, and we for him; and one Lord, Jesus Christ, **through whom are all things, and we live through him**. **7** However, *that knowledge isn't in all men*. But some, with consciousness of an idol until now, eat as of a thing sacrificed to an idol, and their conscience, being weak, is **defiled**. **8** But food will not commend us to God. For neither, if we don't <u>eat</u> are we the worse, nor if we eat are we the better.

NOTE: The spies necessarily ate food that was dedicated to the gods of the land. Caleb rightly understood that God's power was greater than those gods and was willing to go up and possess it in faith. Paul sees parallels in that story to the current Corinthian situation of believers living in a city full of food that was being sacrificed to idols.

Numbers 14	1 Cor. 8:9

Num 14:1 All the congregation lifted up their voice and cried; and the people wept that night. **2** All the children of Israel murmured against Moses and against Aaron. The whole congregation said to them, "We wish that we had died in the land of Egypt, or that we had died in this wilderness! **3 Why does Yahweh bring us to this land, to fall by the sword**? Our wives and our little ones will be captured or killed! Wouldn't it be better for us to return into Egypt?" **4** They said to one another, "Let's choose a leader, and let's return into Egypt." **5** Then Moses and Aaron fell on their faces before all the assembly of the congregation of the children of Israel. **6 <u>Joshua the son of Nun and Caleb the son of Jephunneh</u>**, who were of those who spied out the land, tore their clothes. **7** They spoke to all the congregation of the children of Israel, saying, "The land, which we passed through to spy it out, **is an exceedingly good land**. **8** If Yahweh delights in us, then he will bring us into this land, and give it to us: a land which flows with milk and honey. **9** Only **<u>don't rebel against Yahweh, neither fear the people of the land</u>**; for they are bread for us. Their defense is removed from over them, and Yahweh is with us. Don't fear them." **10** But all the congregation threatened to stone them with stones. The glory of Yahweh appeared in the Tent of Meeting to all the children of Israel.	**1Cor 8:9** But take care that this **liberty of yours doesn't somehow become a stumbling block to the weak**. **10** For if a man sees <u>**you who have knowledge**</u> sitting **in an idol's temple**, won't his conscience, if he is weak, **<u>be emboldened to eat things sacrificed to idols</u>**?

NOTE: The whole congregation has been freed from the slavery of Egypt, but some in that congregation, within the context of that new "liberty" had found an opportunity to complain, pulling the whole congregation down with them. Paul echoes this in 1 Corinthians 8:9. For further explanation of the echo between Canaan and meat sacrificed to idols see the note below 1 Cor. 8:12.

Num 14:11 Yahweh said to Moses, "How long will this people despise me? How long will they not believe in me, for all the signs which I have worked among them? **12** I will **strike them with the pestilence, and disinherit them**, and will make of you a nation greater and mightier than they."

13 Moses said to Yahweh, "Then the Egyptians will hear it; for you brought up this people in your might from among them. **14** They will tell it to the inhabitants of this land. They have heard that you Yahweh are in the middle of this people; for you Yahweh are seen face to face, and your cloud stands over them, and you go before them, in a pillar of cloud by day, and in a pillar of fire by night.

15 Now if you killed this people as one man, then the nations which have heard the fame of you will speak, saying, **16** 'Because Yahweh was not able to bring this people into the land which he swore to them, therefore he has slain them in the wilderness.' **17** Now please let the power of the Lord be great, according as you have spoken, saying, **18** 'Yahweh is slow to anger, and abundant in loving kindness, forgiving iniquity and disobedience; and he will by no means clear the guilty, visiting the iniquity of the fathers on the children, on the third and on the fourth generation.' **19** _Please pardon the iniquity of this people according to the greatness of your loving kindness, and just as you have forgiven this people, from Egypt even until now_."

1Cor 11 And through your knowledge, **he who is weak perishes**, the brother _for whose sake Christ died_.

NOTE: In this great role play, Moses asks God not to allow the weakness of the people to result in their destruction, reminding God of his prior decision to forgive them. God expresses knowledge of their sin to Moses. Moses expresses his knowledge of God back to God. Paul tells the Corinthians that one of the highest callings they can have is to have knowledge of something, and be in the right about it, and yet voluntarily restrain that right for the sake preserving someone else.

Num 14:20 Yahweh said, "I have pardoned according to your word; **21** but in very deed—as I live, and as all the earth shall be filled with Yahweh's glory— **22** because all those men who have seen my glory and my signs, which I worked in Egypt and in the wilderness, yet have tempted me these ten times, and have not listened to my voice; **23** surely they shall not see the land which I swore to their fathers, neither shall any of those who despised me see it. **24** But my servant Caleb, because he had another spirit with him, and has followed me fully, him I will bring into the land into which he went. His offspring shall possess it. **25** Since the Amalekite and the Canaanite dwell in the valley, tomorrow turn, and go into the wilderness by the way to the Red Sea."

26 Yahweh spoke to Moses and to Aaron, saying, **27** "How long shall I bear with this evil congregation that complains against me? I have heard the complaints of the children of Israel, which they complain against me. **28** Tell them, 'As I live, says Yahweh, surely as you have spoken in my ears, so I will do to you. **29** Your dead bodies shall fall in this wilderness; and all who were counted of you, according to your whole number, from twenty years old and upward, who have complained against me, **30** surely you shall not come into the land concerning which I swore that I would make you dwell therein, **except Caleb the son of Jephunneh, and Joshua the son of Nun**. **31** But I will bring in your little ones that you said should be captured or killed, and they shall know the land which you have rejected. **32** But as for you, your dead bodies shall fall in this wilderness. **33** Your children shall be wanderers in the wilderness forty years, and shall bear your prostitution, until your dead bodies are consumed in the wilderness. **34** After the number of the days in which you spied out the land, even forty days, for every day a year, you will bear your iniquities, **even forty years,** and you will know my alienation.' **35** I, Yahweh, have spoken. I will surely do this to all this evil congregation who are gathered together against me. In this wilderness they shall be consumed, and there they shall die."

1Cor 8:12 Thus, sinning against the brothers, and wounding their conscience when it is weak, you sin against Christ. **13** Therefore, **if food causes my brother to stumble**, I will eat no meat **forever** more, that I don't cause my brother to stumble.

NOTE: Paul wraps up his lesson thematically to the whole Numbers 14 incident in 1 Corinthians 8:12-13. The land of Caanan was full of evil and the worship of false gods. Its fruit was harvested under that evil system and was spiritually defiled through pagan rituals. While Joshua and Caleb knew this, they also knew that God's promises were higher and stronger. In Numbers 14:9 they even used a food analogy to express their faith in God, saying to the people, "they are bread for us." Similarly, Paul teaches that while food sacrificed to idols *can* be eaten, it is a sin against Christ to use one's strong faith in a public manner that causes the weak to stumble. Paul teaches that God's will in such a case is *restraint!* That is exactly what Joshua and Caleb did! They did not try to take the promised land on their own. They remained in the camp with those of lesser faith, *restraining themselves forty more years* in the wilderness before taking the land and eating the fruit of the Promised Land again. Paul magnificently writes to the Corinthians that he is willing to wait *forever* if needed.

Num 14:36 The men whom Moses sent to spy out the land, who returned and made all the congregation to murmur against him by bringing up an evil report against the land, **37** even those men who brought up an evil report of the land, died by the plague before Yahweh. **38** But Joshua the son of Nun and Caleb the son of Jephunneh remained alive of those men who went to spy out the land.

39 Moses told these words to all the children of Israel, and the people mourned greatly. **40** They rose up early in the morning and went up to the top of the mountain, saying, "Behold, we are here, and will go up to the place which Yahweh has promised; for we have sinned." **41** Moses said, "Why now do you disobey the commandment of Yahweh, since it shall not prosper? **42** Don't go up, for Yahweh isn't among you; that way you won't be struck down before your enemies. **43** For there the Amalekite and the Canaanite are before you, and you will fall by the sword because you turned back from following Yahweh; therefore Yahweh will not be with you." **44** But they presumed to go up to the top of the mountain. Nevertheless, the ark of Yahweh's covenant and Moses didn't depart out of the camp. **45** Then the Amalekites came down, and the Canaanites who lived in that mountain, and struck them and beat them down even to Hormah.

NOTE: Continuing from the prior note, the last two paragraphs of Numbers 14 reveal the benefits that accrued to Joshua and Caleb in their restraint. Because Paul does not seem to touch on the benefits of such restraint in his letter, no direct echoes are proposed here. However, the benefits of their restraint in Numbers are clear: they lived long lives, became leaders of the people, and ultimately prospered in Promised Land.

Numbers 15

1 Corinthians 9

Num 15:1 Yahweh spoke to Moses, saying, **2** "Speak to the children of Israel, and tell them, 'When you have come into the land of your habitations, which I give to you, **3** and will make an offering by fire to Yahweh—a burnt offering, or a sacrifice, to accomplish a vow, or as a **free will offering**, or in your set feasts, to make a pleasant aroma to Yahweh, of the herd, or of the flock— **4** then **he who offers his offering shall offer to Yahweh** a meal offering of one tenth of an ephah of fine flour mixed with one fourth of a hin of oil. **5** You shall prepare wine for the drink offering, one fourth of a hin, with the burnt offering or for the sacrifice, for each lamb. **6** "'For a ram, you shall prepare for a meal offering two tenths of an ephah of fine flour mixed with the third part of a hin of oil; **7** and for the drink offering you shall offer the third part of a hin of wine, of a pleasant aroma to Yahweh. **8** When you prepare a bull for a burnt offering or for a sacrifice, to accomplish a vow, or for peace offerings to Yahweh, **9** then he shall offer with the bull a meal offering of three tenths of an ephah of fine flour mixed with half a hin of oil; **10** and you shall offer for the drink offering half a hin of wine, for an offering made by fire, of a pleasant aroma to Yahweh.

11 Thus it shall be done for each bull, for each ram, for each of the male lambs, or of the young goats. **12** According to the number that you shall prepare, so you shall do to everyone according to their number. **13** "All who are native-born shall do these things in this way, in offering an offering made by fire, of a pleasant aroma to Yahweh.

1Cor 9:1

Am I not free?

Am I not an apostle?

Haven't **I seen Jesus Christ**, our Lord?

Aren't you my work in the Lord?

2 If to others I am not an apostle,

yet at least I am to you;

for you are the seal of my apostleship in the Lord.

NOTE: Paul's apparent echo of the potential to offer a free will offering in the promised land, being the essence of being "free" is compatible with many New Testament scholars who write that true freedom is not only freedom from sin, but it is the opportunity to do good works in Christ. While in other places "pleasant aroma" is echoed in "Spirit," here it seems that Paul recognizes his apostleship is in fact a "pleasant aroma to Yahweh," a phrase repeated four times in this section.

Num 15:14 If a **stranger lives as a foreigner with you**, or whoever may be among you throughout your generations, and will offer an offering made by fire, of a pleasant aroma to Yahweh, as you do, so he shall do. **15** For the assembly, there shall be one statute for you and for the **stranger who lives as a foreigner**, a statute forever throughout your generations. As you are, so the foreigner shall be before Yahweh. **16** One law and one ordinance shall be for you and for the **stranger who lives as a foreigner** with you.'"

17 Yahweh spoke to Moses, saying, **18** "Speak to the children of Israel, and tell them, 'When you come into the land where I bring you, **19** then it shall be that when you **eat** of the bread of the land, you shall offer up a wave offering to Yahweh. **20** Of the first of your dough you shall offer up a cake for a wave offering. As the wave offering of the threshing floor, so you shall heave it. **21** Of the first of your dough, you shall give to Yahweh a wave offering throughout your generations.

1Cor 9:3 My defense to those who examine me is this:

4 Have we no right to eat and to drink?

5 Have we no right to take along a believing wife, even as the rest of the apostles, and the brothers of the Lord, and Cephas?

6 Or have only Barnabas and I no right to not work?

7 What soldier ever serves at his own expense? Who plants a vineyard, and doesn't **eat** of its fruit? Or who feeds a flock, and doesn't drink from the flock's milk?

NOTE: Three times Paul echoes the situation of a "stranger living as a foreigner" with a defense of the basic rights of those who are sent out by God. Paul's second echo of "stranger who lives as a foreigner with you" in the ability to "take along one's believing wife" might be connected to the phrase "for the assembly" in Numbers 15:14.

NOTE: Paul's phrase "to eat and to drink" in 1 Corinthians 9:4 is echoed in "meal offering and drink offering" Num. 15:24, in the next sectional pairing. John David Pitcher coined the term "pre-echo" for such cases. Generally speaking, the smaller the sectional pairings are constructed, the more likely that pre-echoes and post-echoes will occur. The sectional pairings in the Echoes Bible are formed primarily around topic boundaries, but secondly to attempt a pleasing visual layout in book form.

Num 15:22 "'When you err, and don't observe all these **commandments which Yahweh has spoken to Moses**— 23 even all that Yahweh has commanded you by Moses, from the day that **Yahweh gave commandment and onward throughout your generations**— 24 then it shall be, if it was done unwittingly, without the knowledge of the congregation, that all the congregation shall offer one young bull for a burnt offering, for a pleasant aroma to Yahweh, with its meal offering and its drink offering, according to the ordinance, and one male goat for a sin offering. 25 *The priest shall make atonement for all the congregation of the children of Israel*, and they shall be forgiven; for it was an error, and they **have brought their offering, an offering made by fire to Yahweh**, and their sin offering before Yahweh, for their error. 26 All the congregation of the children of Israel shall be forgiven, as well as the stranger who lives as a foreigner among them; for with regard to all the people, it was done unwittingly.

27 "'If a person *sins* unwittingly, then he shall offer a female goat a year old for a sin offering. 28 The priest shall make atonement for the soul who errs when he *sins* unwittingly before Yahweh. He shall make atonement for him; and he shall be forgiven. 29 You shall have one law for him who *does* anything unwittingly, for him who is native-born among the children of Israel, and for the stranger who lives as a foreigner among them. 30 "'But the soul who *does* anything with **a high hand**, whether he is native-born or a foreigner, *blasphemes* Yahweh. That *soul shall be cut off from* among his people. 31 Because he has *despised* **Yahweh's word**, and has *broken* his commandment, that soul shall be utterly cut off. His *iniquity* shall be on him.'"

1Cor 9:8 Do I speak these things according to the ways of men? Or doesn't the law also say the same thing? **9 For it is written in the law of Moses**, "You shall not muzzle an ox while it treads out the grain." Is it for the oxen that God cares, 10 or does he say it altogether for our sake? **Yes, it was written for our sake**, because he who plows ought to plow in hope, and he who threshes in hope should partake of his hope. 11 If we sowed to you spiritual things, is it a great thing if we reap your fleshly things? 12 If others partake of this right over you, don't we yet more? Nevertheless, we didn't use this right, but we bear all things, that we may cause no hindrance to the *Good News* of Christ. 13 *Don't you know that those who serve around sacred things eat from the things of the temple*, and **those who wait on the altar have their portion with the altar**? 14 Even so the Lord ordained that those who proclaim the Good News should live from the Good News. 15 But I have used none of these things, and I don't write these things that it may be done so in my case; for I would rather die, than that anyone should make my boasting void. 16 For if I preach the Good News, **I have nothing to boast about**, for necessity is laid on me; but **woe is to me** if I don't preach the Good News. 17 For if I do this of my own will, I have a reward. But if not of my own will, I have a **stewardship entrusted to me**. 18 What then is my reward? That when I preach the Good News, I may present the Good News of Christ without charge, so as not to abuse my authority in the *Good News*.

NOTE: Numbers 15:27-31 concludes with 8 references to sin: sins, sins, does anything unwittingly, does anything with a high hand, blasphemes Yahweh, despised Yahweh's word, broken his commandment, and iniquity. Correspondingly, 1 Corinthians 9:12-18 contains 8 mentions of "Good News." Note that 1 Cor. 9:13 echoes a temple sacrifice in Num. 24:25.

Num 15:32 While the children of Israel were in the wilderness, they found a man <u>gathering sticks on the Sabbath</u> day. **33** Those who found him gathering sticks brought him to Moses and Aaron, and to all the congregation. **34 They put him in custody**, because it had not been declared what should be done to him. **35** Yahweh said to Moses, "The man shall surely be put to death.

<u>All the congregation shall stone him</u> with stones outside of the camp." **36 *All the congregation brought him outside of the camp***, and stoned him to death with stones, as Yahweh commanded Moses.

1Cor 9:19 For though I was free from all, **I brought myself under bondage to all**, that I might gain the more.

20 <u>**To the Jews I became as a Jew**</u>, that I might gain Jews; to those who are under the law, as under the law, that I might gain those who are under the law; **21** to those who are without law, as without law (not being without law toward God, but under law toward Christ), that I might gain those who are without law. **22** To the weak I became as weak, that I might gain the weak. *I have become all things to all men, that I may by all means save some*. **23** Now I do this for the sake of the <u>Good News</u>, that I may be a joint partaker of it.

NOTE: It seems that Paul is putting himself into the shoes of the man who was gathering sticks on the Sabbath! Paul writes he brought himself under bondage and willingly took on the consequences. Does Paul see something deeper in the Numbers story that is brilliantly divine, rather than just the tragic consequences of sin? Does Paul see Christ as having *deliberately* put himself into bondage to all Jews by His so-called "breaking" of the Sabbath, and did Christ use it to bring about His own death so that he could gain all? This pairing details exactly one sin in Numbers and mentions "Good News" exactly once.

15:37 Yahweh spoke to Moses, saying, **38** "Speak to the children of Israel, and tell them that they should make themselves fringes on the borders of their garments throughout their generations, and that they put on the fringe of each border a cord of blue. **39** It shall be to you for a fringe, that you may see it, and **remember all Yahweh's commandments**, and do them; and that you <u>**don't follow your own heart and your own eyes**</u>, after which you used to play the prostitute; **40** that you may remember and do all my commandments, and be holy to your God. **41** I am Yahweh your God, who brought you out of the land of Egypt, to be your God: I am Yahweh your God."

1Cor 9:24 Don't you know that those who run in a race all run, but one receives the prize? Run like that, that you may win.

25 Every man who strives in the games **exercises self-control in all things**. Now they do it to receive a corruptible crown, but we an incorruptible. **26** I therefore run like that, not aimlessly. I fight like that, not beating the air, **27** but <u>**I beat my body and bring it into submission**</u>, lest by any means, after I have preached to others, I myself should be disqualified.

NOTE: [Shelach ends.] The echo here is primarily thematic. The Tzitzit on the corners of the garment were to be visible and for remembrance of the keeping of Yahweh's commandments. Correspondingly, Paul speaks of highly visible activities in 1 Corinthians 9:26-27: running, fighting, and preaching, that require self-control and bringing our bodies into submission to a greater purpose. Once again, Paul brilliantly contextualizes God's principles in Numbers into a letter that can be readily understood by the Corinthian church.

Numbers 16

1 Corinthians 10

Num 16:1 Korah, the son of Izhar, the <u>son of Kohath, the son of Levi, with Dathan and Abiram, the sons of Eliab, and On, the son of Peleth, sons of Reuben</u>, took some men. **2** They **rose up before Moses**, with some of the children of Israel, two hundred fifty princes of the congregation, called to the assembly, men of renown. **3** They assembled themselves together against Moses and against Aaron, and said to them, "You take too much on yourself, since all the congregation are holy, every one of them, and Yahweh is among them! Why do you lift yourselves up above Yahweh's assembly?"

4 When Moses heard it, he fell on his face. **5** He said to Korah and to all his company, "In the morning, Yahweh will show who are his, and who is holy, and will cause him to come near to him. The one whom he chooses he will cause to come near to him. **6** Do this: take censers, Korah, and all his company, **7** and put fire in them, and put incense on them before Yahweh tomorrow. It shall be that the man whom Yahweh chooses, he shall be holy. You have gone too far, you sons of Levi!"

1Cor 10:1 Now I would not have you ignorant, **brothers**, that <u>our fathers</u> were all under the cloud, and all passed through the sea; **2** and were all **baptized into Moses** in the cloud and in the sea;

NOTE: [Korach.] Korah and his followers were baptized into Moses in the Red Sea. They went down between the waters, and then rose up again above the waters of the Red Sea.

Num 16:8 Moses said to Korah, "Hear now, you sons of Levi! **9** Is it a small thing to you that the God of Israel has separated you from the congregation of Israel, to bring you near to himself, to do the service of Yahweh's tabernacle, and to stand before the congregation to minister to them, **10** and that he has brought you near, and all your brothers the sons of Levi with you? Do you seek the priesthood also? **11** Therefore you and all your company have gathered together against Yahweh! What is Aaron that you complain against him?"

12 Moses sent to call Dathan and Abiram, the sons of Eliab; and they said, "We won't come up! **13** Is it a small thing that you have brought us up out of a land flowing with milk and honey, to kill us in the wilderness, but you must also make yourself a prince over us? **14** Moreover you haven't brought us into a land flowing with milk and honey, nor given us inheritance of fields and vineyards. Will you put out the eyes of these men? We won't come up!"

16:15 Moses was very angry, and said to Yahweh, "Don't respect their offering. I have not taken one donkey from them, neither have I hurt one of them." **16** Moses said to Korah, "You and all your company go before Yahweh, you, and they, and Aaron, tomorrow. **17** Each man take his censer and put incense on it, and each man bring before Yahweh his censer, two hundred fifty censers; you also, and Aaron, each with his censer." **18** They each took his censer, and put fire in it, and laid incense on it, and stood at the door of the Tent of Meeting with Moses and Aaron. **19** Korah assembled all the congregation against them to the door of the Tent of Meeting. Yahweh's glory appeared to all the congregation.

20 Yahweh spoke to Moses and to Aaron, saying, **21** "Separate yourselves from among this congregation, that I may consume them in a moment!" **22** They fell on their faces, and said, "**God, the God of the spirits of all flesh**, shall one man sin, and will you be angry with all the congregation?"

1**Cor 10:3** and all ate the same spiritual food; **4** and all drank the same spiritual drink.

For they drank of a **spiritual rock that followed them, and the rock was Christ**.

NOTE: Korah and his followers did not appreciate the spiritual food and drink that they had been offered. Instead, they complained that Moses had not provided them a physical food and drink in the new land. It was Moses and Aaron, who would recognize that the God who had not yet given them the "Inheritance of fields they desired" had instead given them himself. So, they fell on their faces and cried out to "God, the God of the spirits of all flesh," who is none other than Christ himself!

Num 16:23 Yahweh spoke to Moses, saying, **24** "Speak to the congregation, saying, 'Get away from around the tent of Korah, Dathan, and Abiram!'"

25 Moses rose up and went to Dathan and Abiram; and the elders of Israel followed him. **26** He spoke to the congregation, saying, "Depart, please, from the tents of these wicked men, and touch nothing of theirs, lest you be consumed in all their sins!" **27** So they went away from the tent of Korah, Dathan, and Abiram, on every side. Dathan and Abiram came out and stood at the door of their tents with their wives, their sons, and their little ones. **28** Moses said, "Hereby you shall know that Yahweh has sent me to do all these works; for I have not done them of my own mind. **29** If these men die the common death of all men, or if they experience what all men experience, then Yahweh hasn't sent me. **30** But if Yahweh makes a new thing, and the ground opens its mouth, and swallows them up with all that belong to them, and they go down alive into Sheol, then you shall understand that these men have despised Yahweh." **31 As he finished speaking all these words, the ground that was under them split apart**. **32** The earth opened its mouth and swallowed them up with their households, all of Korah's men, and all their goods. **33** So they, and all that belonged to them, went down alive into Sheol. The earth closed on them, and they perished from among the assembly. **16:34 All Israel that were around them fled at their cry; for they said, "Lest the earth swallow us up**!" **35 Fire came out from Yahweh and devoured the two hundred fifty men who offered the incense**.

1Cor 10:5 However **with most of them, God was not well pleased, for they were overthrown in the wilderness**.

6 Now these things **were our examples, to the intent we should not lust** after evil things, as they also lusted. **7** Don't be idolaters, as some of them were. As it is written, "The people sat down to eat and drink, and rose up to play." **8** Let's not commit sexual immorality, as some of them committed, and in one day twenty-three thousand fell. **10:9** Let's not test Christ, as some of them tested, and perished by the serpents. **10** Don't grumble, as some of them also grumbled and perished by the destroyer.

NOTE: 1 Corinthians 10:7-10 detail two additional, better-known examples on the same topic. 1 Cor. 10:7-8 clearly refer to the golden calf incident while 1 Cor. 10:9-10 look ahead to Numbers Ch. 21, which tells the story of the fiery serpents. A reasonable question here is: why didn't Paul just wait until Numbers 21 to speak against grumblers? Possibly because Paul decided to use the fiery serpent story to speak against factions and the improper dividing of his body as leading to weakness, sickness and even death. Paul had other business to attend to regarding Corinth, and Numbers Ch. 21 would be the best place to do it.

Num 16:36 Yahweh spoke to Moses, saying, **37** "Speak to Eleazar the son of Aaron the priest, that he take up the censers out of the burning, and scatter the fire away from the camp; for they are holy, **38** even the censers of these **sinners against their own lives. Let them be made beaten plates for a covering of the altar**, for they offered them before Yahweh. Therefore, they are holy. **They shall be a sign to the children of Israel**." **39** Eleazar the priest took the bronze censers which those who were burned had offered; and they beat them out for a covering of the altar, **40** to be **a memorial to the children of Israel**, to the end that no stranger who isn't of the seed of Aaron, would come near to burn incense before Yahweh, that he not be as Korah and as his company, as Yahweh spoke to him by Moses.

1Cor 10:11 Now all these things **happened to them by way of example**,

and they were **written for our admonition**,

on whom the ends of the ages have come.

NOTE: While the story of Korah is difficult to hear, Paul states that it was written for our admonition, in other words that we might not make the same mistakes. Is it possible that the testimony of those who lose their lives at the hand of God in cases such as this, might one day include an accounting from God of those who did not sin as they did, because their gut-wrenching account was "written for our admonition"? If true, the best thing we can do for those who died is to not make the same mistakes, thanking God for their counterexample, and admitting 'there but for the grace of God go I'.

Num 16:41 But on the next day all the congregation of the **children of Israel complained against Moses and against Aaron, saying, "You have killed Yahweh's people!"**

1Cor 10:12 Therefore **let him who thinks he stands be careful that he doesn't fall**.

NOTE: The people in Numbers 16:41 may have thought they were taking a righteous stand, but they would soon fall. In reality they were taking up an offense at both Moses and God.

Num 16:42 When the congregation was assembled against Moses and against Aaron, they looked toward the Tent of Meeting. Behold, the **cloud covered it, and Yahweh's glory appeared**. **43** Moses and Aaron came to the front of the Tent of Meeting. **44** Yahweh spoke to Moses, saying, **45** "Get away from among this congregation, that I may consume them in a moment!" They fell on their faces. **46** Moses said to Aaron, "Take your censer, put fire from the altar in it, lay incense on it, carry it quickly to the congregation, and make atonement for them; for wrath has gone out from Yahweh! The plague has begun." **47** Aaron did as Moses said and ran into the middle of the assembly. <u>**The plague had already begun among the people. He put on the incense and made atonement for the people.**</u> <u>**48 He stood between the dead and the living; and the plague was stayed**</u>. **49** Those who died by the plague were fourteen thousand seven hundred, besides those who died about the matter of Korah. **50** Aaron returned to Moses to the door of the Tent of Meeting, **and the plague was stopped**.

1Cor 10:13 No temptation has taken you except what is common to man. **God is faithful**, who will not allow you to be tempted above what you are able, but will with the temptation **also <u>make the way of escape</u>**, that you may **be able to endure it**.

NOTE: The echo of 1 Corinthians 10:13 with the passage can be understood in two potential ways. First this verse echoes all of Numbers 16:42-50, in the sense that Paul was reasoning that the plague was not inevitable! There *was* a way of escape for the people not to take offense at the situation. The second way to understand this passage is a beautiful thought conveyed in the echo of the phrase "also made the way of escape" which echoes the atonement made for the people after they sinned. In this sense, could it be that the "way of escape" intended by Paul is actually a way of escape *after* we fall to the temptation, and *then fall into the sin itself*? This is exactly the situation in Num. 16:42-50! The people had a way of escape but took offense and fell into sin. But God then provided a way of escape from the consequence of their sin (the plague) and the damage from the plague was minimized.

Numbers 17	1 Cor. 10:14

Num 17:1 Yahweh spoke to Moses, saying, **2** "Speak to the children of Israel, and take rods from them, one for each fathers' house, of all their princes according to their fathers' houses, twelve rods. Write each man's name on his rod. **3 You shall write Aaron's name on the rod of Levi; for there shall be one rod for each head of their fathers' houses**. **4** You shall lay them up in the Tent of Meeting before the covenant, where I meet with you. **5** It shall happen that the **rod of the man whom I shall choose shall bud**. I will make the murmurings of the children of Israel, which they murmur against you, to cease from me." **6** Moses spoke to the children of Israel; and all their princes gave him rods, for each prince one, according to their fathers' houses, even twelve rods. Aaron's rod was among their rods. **7** Moses laid up the rods before Yahweh in the Tent of the Testimony.

8 The next day Moses went into the Tent of the Testimony; and behold, Aaron's rod for the house of Levi had sprouted, <u>budded</u>, blossomed, and produced almonds. **9** Moses brought out all the rods from before Yahweh to all the children of Israel. They looked, **and each man took his rod**. **10** Yahweh said to Moses, "Put back the rod of Aaron before the covenant, to be kept as a token against the rebels; that you may make an end of their murmurings against me, that they not die." **11** Moses did so. As Yahweh commanded him, so he did.

12 The children of Israel spoke to Moses, saying, "Behold, we perish! We are undone! We are all undone! **13** Everyone who comes near, who comes near to the **tabernacle of Yahweh, dies**! Will we all perish?"

1**Cor 10:14** Therefore, my beloved, flee from idolatry. **15 I speak as to wise men**. Judge what I say. **16** <u>The cup of blessing which we bless</u>, isn't it a sharing of the <u>blood</u> of Christ? **<u>The bread which we break</u>**, isn't it a sharing of the **body of Christ**?

NOTE: It seems that the best parallelism in this section is that the bread we break echoes the each man's rod, the cup of blessing echoes the rod of the man that buds, and the wine in that cup (i.e. the blood) echoes the "budded, blossomed and produced almonds." Echoes 2, 3 and 4 are presented as an idea only, and require further study. Echoes 1 and 5 seem reasonable.

Numbers 18

1 Corinthians 10:17

Num 18:1 Yahweh said to Aaron, "You and your sons and your fathers' house with you shall bear the iniquity of the sanctuary; and you and your sons with you shall bear the iniquity of your priesthood. **2 Bring your brothers also, the tribe of Levi, the tribe of your father, near with you, that they may be joined to you, and minister to you; but you and your sons with you shall be before the Tent of the Testimony.** 3 They shall keep your commands and the duty of the whole Tent; only they shall not come near to the vessels of the sanctuary and to the altar, that they not die, neither they nor you. 4 They shall be joined to you and keep the responsibility of the Tent of Meeting, for all the service of the Tent. A stranger shall not come near to you.

1Cor 10:17 Because there is one loaf of bread, we, who are many, are one body; for we all partake of the one loaf of bread.

NOTE: The unity here, the "one loaf of bread," is between the priesthood and the rest of the Levites.

Num 18:5 "You shall perform the duty of the sanctuary and the duty of the altar, that there be no more wrath on the **children of Israel**. 6 Behold, I myself have taken your brothers the Levites from among the children of Israel. To you they are a gift, given to Yahweh, to do the service of the Tent of Meeting. 7 You and your sons with you shall keep your **priesthood for everything of the altar,** *and for that within the veil*. You shall serve. I give you the priesthood as a service of gift. The **stranger who comes near shall be put to death**."

1Cor 10:18 Consider Israel according to the flesh. **Don't those who eat the sacrifices participate in the altar**? 19 What am I saying then? That a thing sacrificed to idols is anything, or that an idol is anything? **20** But I say that the things which the Gentiles sacrifice, they sacrifice to demons and not to God, and I don't desire that you would have fellowship with demons. **21 *You can't both drink the cup of the Lord and the cup of demons*.** You can't both partake of the Lord's table and of the table of demons. **22 Or do we provoke the Lord to jealousy? Are we stronger than he**?

NOTE: The service of the Tent includes, of course, the participation in the sacrifices in the altar. It is impossible for demons to be present behind the veil in the Holy of Holies. In the same way there is no fellowship in the cup of the Lord and with demons, and to attempt it – whatever that looks like -- according to Num. 18:7 is to invite death.

Num 18:8 Yahweh spoke to Aaron, "Behold, I myself have given you the command of my wave offerings, even all the holy things of the children of Israel. I have given them to you by reason of the anointing, and to your sons, as a portion forever. **9 This shall be yours** of the most holy things from the fire: every offering of theirs, even every meal offering of theirs, and every sin offering of theirs, and every trespass offering of theirs, which they shall render to me, shall be most holy for you and for your sons. **10** You shall eat of it like the most holy things. Every male shall eat of it. It shall be holy to you. **11** "This is yours, too: the wave offering of their gift, even all the wave **offerings of the children of Israel**. I have given them to you, and to your sons and to your daughters with you, as a portion forever. Everyone who is clean in your house shall eat of it. **12** *"I have given to you all the best of the oil, all the best of the vintage, and of the grain, the first fruits of them which they give to Yahweh*. **13** The first-ripe fruits of all that is in their land, which they bring to Yahweh, shall be yours. Everyone who is clean in your house shall eat of it. **14** "Everything devoted in Israel shall be yours. **15** Everything that opens the womb, of all flesh which they offer to Yahweh, both of man and animal, shall be yours. Nevertheless, you shall surely redeem the firstborn of man, and you shall redeem the firstborn of unclean animals. **16** You shall redeem those who are to be redeemed of them from a month old, according to your estimation, for five shekels of money, according to the shekel of the sanctuary, which weighs twenty gerahs. **17** "But you shall not redeem the firstborn of a cow, or the firstborn of a sheep, or the firstborn of a goat. They are holy. You shall sprinkle their blood on the altar and shall burn their fat for an offering made by fire, for a pleasant aroma to Yahweh. **18** Their meat shall be yours, as the wave offering breast and as the right thigh, it shall be yours. **19** All the wave offerings of the holy things, which the children of Israel offer to Yahweh, have I given you and your sons and your daughters with you, as a portion forever. It is a covenant of salt forever before Yahweh to you and to your offspring with you." **20** Yahweh said to Aaron, "You shall have no inheritance in their land, neither shall you have any portion among them. **I am your portion and your inheritance among the children of Israel**.

1Cor 10:23 "**All things are lawful for me," but not all things are profitable**. "All things are lawful for me," but not all things build up. **24** Let no one seek his own, **but each one his neighbor's good**. **25** Whatever is sold in the meat market, eat, asking no question for the sake of conscience, **26** *for "the earth is the Lord's, and its fullness*."

NOTE: 1 Corinthians 10:26 should apply to all the tribes. For most tribes, its echo is found in Numbers 18:12, but for the tribe of Levi it is found in Num. 18:20. Perhaps Levi received the best inheritance of all, because their fullness is the Lord himself.

Num 18:21 "**To the children of Levi, behold, I have given all the tithe in Israel for an inheritance**, in return for their service which they serve, even the service of the Tent of Meeting. **22** Henceforth the children of Israel shall not come near the Tent of Meeting, lest they bear sin, and die. **23** <u>But the Levites shall do the service of the Tent of Meeting, and they shall bear their iniquity</u>. It shall be a statute forever throughout your generations. Among the children of Israel, they shall have no inheritance. **24** For the tithe of the children of Israel, which they offer as a wave offering to Yahweh, I have given to the Levites for an inheritance. Therefore, I have said to them, 'Among the children of Israel they shall have no inheritance.'"

25 Yahweh spoke to Moses, saying, **26** "Moreover you shall speak to the Levites, and tell them, 'When you take of the children of Israel the tithe which I have given you from them for your inheritance, then you shall offer up a wave offering of it for Yahweh, a tithe of the tithe. **27** *Your wave offering shall be credited to you, as though it were the grain of the threshing floor, and as the fullness of the wine press*. **28** Thus you also shall offer a wave offering to Yahweh of all your tithes, which you receive of the children of Israel; and of it you shall give Yahweh's wave offering to Aaron the priest. **29** Out of all your gifts, you shall offer every wave offering of Yahweh, of all its best parts, even the holy part of it.' **30** "Therefore you shall tell them, 'When you heave its best from it, <u>then it shall be credited to the Levites</u> as the increase of the threshing floor, and as the increase of the wine press. **31** You may eat it anywhere, you and your households, for it is your reward in return for your service in the Tent of Meeting. **32** **You shall bear no sin by reason of it, when you have heaved from it its best**. You shall not profane the holy things of the children of Israel, that you not die.'"

1Cor 10:27 If one of those who don't believe invites you to a meal, and you are inclined to go, **eat whatever is set before you, asking no questions** for the sake of conscience. **28** <u>But if anyone says to you, "This was offered to idols," don't eat it</u> for the sake of the one who told you, and for the sake of conscience.

For "the earth is the Lord's, and all its fullness."

29 Conscience, I say, not your own, but the other's conscience. <u>For why is my liberty judged by another</u> conscience? **30** If I partake with thankfulness, **why am I denounced for that for which I give thanks**?

NOTE: [Korach ends.]

Numbers 19	1 Corinthians 10:31
Num 19:1 Yahweh spoke to Moses and to Aaron, saying, **2** "This is the statute of the law which Yahweh has commanded. Tell the children of Israel to bring you a red heifer without spot, in which is no defect, and which was never yoked. **3** You shall give her to Eleazar the priest, and he shall bring her outside of the camp, and one shall kill her before his face. **4 Eleazar the priest shall take some of her blood with his finger, and sprinkle her blood toward the front of the Tent of Meeting seven times**. **5** One shall burn the heifer in his sight; her skin, and her meat, and her blood, with her dung, shall he burn.	**1Cor 10:31** Whether therefore you eat or drink, or whatever you do, **do all to the glory of God**.

NOTE: [Chukat.]

Num 19:6 The **priest** shall take cedar wood, hyssop, and scarlet, and cast it into the middle of the burning of the heifer. **7** Then the priest shall wash his clothes, and he shall bathe his flesh in water, and afterward he shall come into the camp, and the priest shall be unclean until the evening. **8** He who burns her shall wash his clothes in water, and bathe his flesh in water, and shall be unclean until the evening. **9** "A **man** who is clean shall gather up the ashes of the heifer and lay them up outside of the camp in a clean place; and it shall be kept for the **congregation of the children of Israel** for a water for impurity. It is a sin offering. **10** He who gathers the ashes of the heifer shall wash his clothes and be unclean until the evening. It shall be to the children of Israel, and to the stranger who lives as a foreigner among them, for a statute forever. **11** "He who touches the dead body of any man shall be unclean seven days. **12** He shall purify himself with the water on the third day, and on the seventh day he shall be clean; but if he doesn't purify himself the third day, then the seventh day he shall not be clean	**1Cor 10:32** Give no occasion for stumbling, either to **Jews**, or to **Greeks**, or to the **assembly of God**;

Num 19:13 Whoever **touches a dead person, the body of a man who has died, and doesn't purify himself, defiles Yahweh's tabernacle**; and that soul shall be cut off from Israel; because the water for impurity was not sprinkled on him, he shall be unclean. His uncleanness is yet on him.

14 "This is the law when a man dies in a tent: everyone who comes into the tent, and everyone who is in the tent, shall be unclean seven days. **15** Every open vessel, which has no covering bound on it, is unclean. **16** "Whoever in the open field touches one who is slain with a sword, or a dead body, or a bone of a man, or a grave, shall be unclean seven days. **17** "For the unclean, they shall take of the ashes of the burning of the sin offering; and running water shall be poured into a vessel. **18** A clean person shall take hyssop, dip it in the water, and sprinkle it on the tent, on all the vessels, on the persons who were there, and on him who touched the bone, or the slain, or the dead, or the grave. **19** <u>The clean person shall sprinkle on the unclean on the third day</u>, and on the seventh day. **On the seventh day, he shall purify him. He shall wash his clothes and bathe himself in water and shall be clean at evening**.

20 But the man who shall be unclean, and shall not purify himself, that soul shall be cut off from among the assembly, because he has defiled the sanctuary of Yahweh. The water for impurity has not been sprinkled on him. He is unclean. **21** It shall be a perpetual statute to them. He who sprinkles the water for impurity shall wash his clothes, and he who touches the water for impurity shall be unclean until evening. **22** Whatever the unclean person touches shall be unclean; and the soul that touches it shall be unclean until evening."

1Cor 10:33 even as I also **please all men** in all things,

 <u>**not seeking my own profit, but the profit of the many**</u>,

that they may be saved.

NOTE: When Paul writes "I also please all me in all things," he may be touching prophetically on his later attempt in Jerusalem to follow the temple regulations, doing everything he could do to meet the purification requirements. The words in Numbers "touches a dead person, the body of a man who has died," reminds us of Paul's earlier words in 1 Cor. 2:2, "For I determined to know nothing among you except Jesus Christ, and him crucified." While Paul's eventual Jerusalem visit sent him to Rome in chains, his goal of "not seeking my own profit, but the profit of the many" was certainly fulfilled in the writings that followed from that event.

Numbers 20   1 Corinthians 11

Num 20:1 The children of Israel, even the whole congregation, came into the wilderness of Zin in the first month. **The people stayed in Kadesh**. Miriam died there and was buried there.

2 There was no water for the congregation, and they assembled themselves together against Moses and against Aaron. **3** The people quarreled with Moses, and spoke, saying, "We wish that we had died when our brothers died before Yahweh! **4** Why have you brought Yahweh's assembly into this wilderness, that we should die there, we and our animals? **5** Why have you made us to come up out of Egypt, to bring us into this evil place? It is no place of seed, or of figs, or of vines, or of pomegranates; neither is there any water to drink." **6 Moses and Aaron went from the presence of the assembly to the door of the Tent of Meeting, and fell on their faces. Yahweh's glory appeared to them.** **7** Yahweh spoke to Moses, saying,

1Cor 11:1 Be imitators of me, even as I also am of Christ.

2 Now I praise you, brothers, that you remember me in all things, and **hold firm the traditions**, even as I delivered them to you. **3** But I would have you know that **the head of every man is Christ**, and the head of the woman is man, **and the head of Christ is God**.

NOTE: Numbers 20:6 shows Moses and Aaron falling on their faces at the door of the Tent of Meeting, the place in which God (in the form of Christ) spoke to Moses face-to-face. The phrase "Yahweh's glory appeared to them" seems to echo "the head of Christ is God" because it calls to mind God showing his glory to Moses in Exodus 33.

Num 20:8 "Take the rod, and assemble the congregation, you, and Aaron your brother, and **speak to the rock before their eyes**, that it give forth its water. You shall bring water to them out of the rock; so you shall give the congregation and their livestock drink."

9 Moses took the rod from before Yahweh, as he commanded him. **10** Moses and Aaron gathered the assembly together before the rock, and he said to them, "Hear now, you rebels! Shall we bring water out of this rock for you?" **11** Moses lifted up his hand, and struck the rock with his rod twice, and water came out abundantly. The congregation and their livestock drank. **12** Yahweh said to Moses and Aaron, "Because you didn't believe in me, to sanctify me in the eyes of the children of Israel, therefore you shall not bring this assembly into the land which I have given them." **13** These are the waters of Meribah; because the children of Israel strove with Yahweh, and he was sanctified in them.

1Cor 11:4 Every man praying or prophesying, having his head covered, dishonors his head.

NOTE: Moses was asked to "speak to the rock before their eyes" but instead called them rebels and took upon himself the authority of bringing out the water. Rather than speaking to the rock, he lifted up his hand and struck it twice. Was Moses in some manner "covering his head" because he lifted up his hand?

Num 20:14 Moses sent messengers from Kadesh to the king of Edom, saying: "Thus says your brother Israel: You know all the travail that has happened to us; **15** how our fathers went down into Egypt, and we lived in Egypt a long time. The Egyptians mistreated us and our fathers. **16** When we cried to Yahweh, he heard our voice, sent an angel, and brought us out of Egypt. Behold, we are in Kadesh, a city in the edge of your border. **17** "Please let us pass through your land. We will not pass through field or through vineyard, neither will we drink from the water of the wells. We will go along the king's highway. We will not turn aside to the right hand nor to the left, until we have passed your border."

18 Edom said to him, "You shall not pass through me, lest I come out with the sword against you." **19** The children of Israel said to him, "We will go up by the highway; and if we drink your water, I and my livestock, then I will give its price. Only let me, without doing anything else, pass through on my feet." **20** He said, "You shall not pass through." **Edom came out** against him with many people, and with a strong hand. **21** Thus Edom refused to give Israel passage through his border, so Israel turned away from him.

1**Cor 11:5** But every woman praying or prophesying with her head uncovered dishonors her head. For it is one and the same thing as if she were shaved. **6** For if a woman is not covered, let her hair also be cut off. But if it is shameful for a woman to have her hair cut off or be shaved, let her be covered. **7** For a man indeed ought not to have his head covered, because he is the image and glory of God, but the woman is the glory of the man. **8** For man is not from woman, but woman from man; **9** for man wasn't created for the woman, but woman for the man. **10** For this cause the woman ought to have authority over her own head, because of the angels. **11** **Nevertheless, neither is the woman independent of the man, nor the man independent of the woman, in the Lord**. **12** For as woman came from man, so a man also comes through a woman; but all things are from God.

NOTE: The echo between Numbers and 1 Corinthians must be taken as a whole concept. Israel is approaching Edom with care and respect, even as Paul is exhorting women to do by covering their heads. Edom is acting in authority over Israel, as if Israel was a woman. The echo to Paul's writings comes from the story of the brothers: of Jacob who favored Rebecca and of Esau who favored his father Isaac. Isaac (by way of Edom) and Rebecca by way of Jacob/Israel) are the man and woman. However, Paul constrains the teaching with the truth that Israel is Isaac's son, and Edom's mother is Rebecca, and that all things are from God.

Num 20:22 They traveled from Kadesh, and the **children of Israel**, even the whole congregation, came to Mount Hor.

23 Yahweh spoke to Moses and Aaron in Mount Hor, by the border of the land of Edom, saying, **24** "**Aaron** shall be gathered to his people; for he shall not enter into the land which I have given to the children of Israel, because you rebelled against my word at the waters of **Meribah**. **25** Take Aaron and Eleazar his son and bring them up to Mount Hor. **26** Strip Aaron of his garments, and put them on Eleazar his son. Aaron shall be gathered and shall die there." **27** Moses did as Yahweh commanded. They went up onto Mount Hor in the sight of all the congregation. **28** Moses stripped Aaron of his garments and put them on Eleazar his son. Aaron died there on the top of the mountain, and Moses and Eleazar came down from the mountain. **29** When all the congregation saw that Aaron was dead, they **wept for Aaron thirty days**, even all the house of Israel.

Numbers 21

21:1 The Canaanite, the king of Arad, who lived in the South, heard that Israel came by the way of Atharim. He fought against Israel and took some of them captive. **2** Israel vowed a vow to Yahweh, and said, "If you will indeed deliver this people into my hand, then I will utterly destroy their cities." **3** Yahweh listened to the voice of **Israel**, and delivered up the Canaanites; and they utterly destroyed them and their cities. The name of the place was called Hormah.

1Cor 11:13 Judge **for yourselves**. Is it appropriate that a woman pray to God unveiled? **14** Doesn't even nature itself teach you that if a man has long hair, it is a dishonor to him? **15** But if a woman has long hair, it is a glory to her, for her hair is given to her for a covering. **11:16** But if any **man** seems to be **contentious**, we have no such **custom**, neither do **God's assemblies**.

NOTE: Meribah means *contention* or *strife*. The death of Aaron initiated a new custom in Jewish life of mourning for thirty days after death. If this is the correct echo, then Paul is saying that regardless of contentious circumstances surrounding a person's death, their death must still be treated with utmost respect.

NOTE: A second possibility is that "contentious" refers to the kind of Arad. If this is the correct echo, then Israel had no such custom to allow contentious behavior including the taking of hostages, and therefore Israel utterly destroyed them. In this case Paul is saying that his leadership team has no custom to tolerate aggressive, contentious behavior, and neither should other assemblies.

Numbers 21:4	1 Corinthians 11:16
Num 21:4 They traveled from Mount Hor by the way to the Red Sea, to go around the land of Edom. The **soul of the people was very discouraged** because of the journey. **5** The **people spoke against God** and against <u>Moses</u>: "Why have you **brought us up out of Egypt** to die in the wilderness? For there is **no bread**, there is no *water*, and our soul loathes this **disgusting** food!"	1**Cor 11:17** But in giving you this command, I don't praise you, that you **come together not for the better but for the worse**. **18** For first of all, when you come together in the assembly, I hear that **divisions exist among you**, and I partly believe it. **19** For there also must be factions among you, that <u>those who are approved may be revealed among you</u>. **20** When therefore you assemble yourselves together, it is not the **Lord's supper that you eat**. **21** For in your eating each one takes his own supper first. One is **hungry**, and another is drunken. **22** What, don't you have houses to eat and to *drink* in? Or do you **despise** God's assembly and put them to shame who don't have anything? What shall I tell you? Shall I praise you? In this I don't praise you.

NOTE: The reason that "brought us up out of Egypt," echoes "Lord's supper that we eat," is that the original Lord's supper was part of the Passover.

Num 21:6 Yahweh sent venomous snakes among the people, and they bit the people. Many people of Israel died. **7** The people came to Moses, and said, "**We have sinned, because we have spoken against Yahweh and against you**. Pray to Yahweh, that he take away the snakes from us." Moses prayed for the people. **8** Yahweh said to Moses, "Make a venomous snake, and set it on a pole. It shall happen that everyone who is bitten, **when he sees it, shall live**." **9** Moses made a snake of bronze, and set it on the pole. **If a snake bit any man**, when he looked at the bronze snake, he lived.

1Cor 11:23 For I received from the Lord that which also I delivered to you, that the Lord Jesus on the night in which he was betrayed took bread. **24** When he had given thanks, he broke it and said, "Take, eat. This is my body, which is broken for you. Do this in memory of me." **25** In the same way he also took the cup, after supper, saying, "This cup is the new covenant in my blood. Do this, as often as you drink, in memory of me." **26** For as often as you eat this bread and drink this cup, you proclaim the Lord's death until he comes.

27 Therefore whoever eats this bread or drinks the Lord's cup in a way unworthy of the Lord will be guilty of the body and the blood of the Lord. **28 But let a man examine himself** and so let him eat of the bread and drink of the cup. **29** For he who eats and drinks in an unworthy way eats and drinks **judgment to himself, if he doesn't discern the Lord's body**. **30** For this cause **many among you are weak and sickly, and not a few sleep**. **31** For if we discerned ourselves, we wouldn't be judged. **32** But when we are judged, we are disciplined by the Lord, that we may not be condemned with the world.

NOTE: The story of the bronze serpent has long been associated with Christ's being lifted up. Here Paul ties it to the Lord's supper and fittingly reasons that factions in the church are dangerous to members' health even as it was in this story of God's response to the Children of Israel.

Num 21:10 The children of Israel **traveled and encamped** in Oboth. **11** They **traveled from Oboth, and encamped** at Iyeabarim, in the wilderness which is before Moab, toward the sunrise. **12** From there they **traveled and encamped** in the valley of Zered. **13** From there they **traveled, and encamped** on the other side of the Arnon, which is in the wilderness that comes out of the border of the Amorites; for the Arnon is the border of Moab, between Moab and the Amorites. **14** Therefore it is said in The Book of the Wars of Yahweh, "Vaheb in Suphah, the valleys of the Arnon, **15** the slope of the valleys that incline toward the dwelling of Ar, leans on the border of Moab." **16** From there they **traveled** to Beer; that is the well where Yahweh said to Moses, "**Gather the people together, and I will give them water**."

17 Then Israel sang this song: "Spring up, well! Sing to it, **18** the well, which the princes dug, which the nobles of the people dug, with the scepter, and with their poles." From the wilderness they **traveled** to Mattanah; **19** and from Mattanah to Nahaliel; and from Nahaliel to Bamoth; **20** and from Bamoth to the valley that is in the field of Moab, to the top of Pisgah, which looks down on the desert.

1Cor 11:33 Therefore, my brothers,

when you come together to eat, wait for one another.

NOTE: The Children of Israel were learning to travel together, come together in the encampments, and to wait for one another. Paul in 1 Corinthians 11:33 echoes this whole set of verses.

Num 21:21 Israel sent messengers to Sihon king of the Amorites, saying, **22** "Let me pass through your land. We will not turn into field or vineyard. We will not drink of the water of the wells. We will go by the king's highway, until we have passed your border." **23** Sihon would not allow Israel to pass through his border, but Sihon gathered all his people together, and went out against Israel into the wilderness, and came to Jahaz. He fought against Israel. **24** Israel struck him with the edge of the sword and possessed his land from the Arnon to the Jabbok, even to the children of Ammon; for the border of the children of Ammon was strong. **25** Israel took all these cities. Israel lived in all the cities of the Amorites, in Heshbon, and in all its villages. **26** For Heshbon was the city of Sihon the king of the Amorites, who had fought against the former king of Moab, and taken all his land out of his hand, even to the Arnon. **27** Therefore those who speak in proverbs say, "Come to Heshbon.

Let the city of Sihon be built and established; **28** for a fire has gone out of Heshbon, a flame from the city of Sihon. It has devoured Ar of Moab, The lords of the high places of the Arnon. **29** **Woe to you, Moab! You are undone**, people of Chemosh! He has given his sons as fugitives, and his daughters into captivity, to Sihon king of the Amorites. **30** We have shot at them. Heshbon has perished even to Dibon. We have laid waste even to Nophah, which reaches to Medeba."

31 Thus Israel lived in the land of the Amorites. **32** Moses sent to spy out Jazer. They took its villages and drove out the Amorites who were there.

33 They turned and went up by the way of Bashan. Og the king of Bashan went out against them, he and all his people, to battle at Edrei. **34** Yahweh said to Moses, "Don't fear him, for I have delivered him into your hand, with all his people, and his land. You shall do to him as you did to Sihon king of the Amorites, who lived at Heshbon." **35** So they struck him, with his sons and all his people, until there was no remnant left him. They possessed his land.

Numbers 22

22:1 The children of Israel traveled and encamped in the plains of Moab beyond the Jordan at Jericho.

1Cor 11:34 But if anyone is hungry, let him eat at home, lest your coming together **be for judgment**.

The rest I will set in order whenever I come.

NOTE: [Chukat ends.] Once they reached the Jordan at Jericho the travels ceased, and Moses would write Deuteronomy that would essentially "set in order" the teachings of the Children of Israel before they crossed into the promised land. Paul may have echoed this idea.

Numbers 22:2	1 Corinthians 12
Num 22:2 Balak the son of Zippor saw all that Israel had done to the Amorites. **3** Moab was very afraid of the people, because they were many. Moab was distressed because of the children of Israel. **4** Moab said to the elders of Midian, "Now this multitude will lick up all that is around us, as the ox licks up the grass of the field." Balak the son of Zippor was king of Moab at that time. **5** He sent messengers to Balaam the son of Beor, to Pethor, which is by the River, to the land of the children of his people, to call him, saying, "Behold, there is a people who came out of Egypt. Behold, they cover the surface of the earth, and they are staying opposite me. **6** Please come now therefore and **curse this people** for me; for they are too mighty for me. Perhaps I shall prevail, that we may strike them, and that I may drive them out of the land; **for I know that he whom you bless is blessed**, and he whom you curse is cursed."	**1Cor 12:1** Now concerning **spiritual things**, brothers, **I don't want you to be ignorant**.

NOTE: [Balak.] The entire narrative now shifts in both Numbers and 1 Corinthians. While Paul begins to address spiritual gifts, Balak launches a plan to engage in "spiritual" warfare against the nation of Israel.

Num 22:7 The elders of Moab and the elders of Midian **departed with the rewards** of **divination** in their hand. They came to Balaam and spoke to him the words of Balak.	**1Cor 12:2** You know that when you were **heathen**, you were **led away** to those **mute idols**, however you might be led.

Num 22:8 He said to them, "Lodge here this night, and I will bring you word again, as Yahweh shall speak to me." The princes of Moab stayed with Balaam.

9 God came to **Balaam**, and said, "Who are these men with you?" **10** Balaam said to God, "Balak the son of Zippor, king of Moab, has said to me, **11** 'Behold, the people that has come out of Egypt covers the surface of the earth. Now, come curse them for me. Perhaps I shall be able to fight against them and shall drive them out.'" **12** <u>God said to Balaam</u>, "You shall not go with them. *You shall not curse the people,* for they are blessed." **13** Balaam rose up in the morning, and said to the princes of Balak, "Go to your land; for Yahweh refuses to permit me to go with you." **14** The princes of Moab rose up, and they went to Balak, and said, "Balaam refuses to come with us."

15 Balak again sent princes, more, and more honorable than they. **16** They came to Balaam, and said to him, "Thus says Balak the son of Zippor, 'Please let nothing hinder you from coming to me, **17** for I will promote you to very great honor, and whatever you say to me I will do. Please come therefore and curse this people for me.'" **18** <u>Balaam answered</u> the servants of Balak, "If Balak would give me his house full of silver and gold, I can't go beyond the **word of Yahweh my God**, to do less or more. **19** Now therefore please stay here tonight as the others did, that I may know what else Yahweh will speak to me." **20** God came to Balaam at night, and said to him, "If the men have come to call you, rise up, go with them; but <u>only the word which I speak</u> to you, that you shall do."

21 Balaam rose up in the morning, and saddled his donkey, and went with the princes of Moab.

1Cor 12:3 Therefore I make known to you that no **man**

<u>speaking by God's Spirit</u> says,

"*Jesus is accursed*."

No **<u>one can say</u>**, "

Jesus is Lord," except by the

<u>Holy Spirit</u>.

NOTE: While the phrase "curse the people" in Numbers 22:12 being suggested to be an echo of "Jesus is accursed," might seem to be a stretch, note that in Num. 22:8 Balaam's phrase "I will <u>bring you word</u>" (*shuv dabar* in Hebrew) could allude to the Jesus as the Living Word being brought forth by God to those who need salvation. The word *dabar* occurs eight times in the full account of Balaam, a number often associated with the work of Christ.

NOTE: In Num. 22:18 the phrase "word of Yahweh my God" echoes "Jesus is Lord," but this statement was spoken by Balaam. In Num. 22:20 the phrase "only the word which I speak" is echoed by "Holy Spirit" because this time God is speaking to Balaam directly.

Num 22:22 God's anger burned because he went; and Yahweh's angel placed himself in the way as an adversary against him. Now he was riding on his donkey, and his two servants were with him. **23** The donkey saw Yahweh's angel standing in the way, with his sword drawn in his hand; and the **donkey turned aside out of the way and went into the field**. Balaam struck the donkey, to turn her into the way. **24** Then Yahweh's angel stood in a narrow path between the vineyards, a wall being on this side, and a wall on that side. **25** The donkey saw Yahweh's angel, **and she thrust herself to the wall, and crushed Balaam's foot against the wall**. He struck her again. **26** Yahweh's angel went further, and stood in a narrow place, where there was no way to turn either to the right hand or to the left. **27** The donkey saw Yahweh's angel, **and she lay down under Balaam**. Balaam's anger burned, and he struck the donkey with his staff. **28** <u>Yahweh opened the mouth of the donkey</u>, and she said to Balaam, "What have I done to you, that you have struck me <u>these three times</u>?" **29** Balaam said to the donkey, "Because you have mocked me, I wish there were a sword in my hand, for now I would have killed you." **30** The donkey said to Balaam, "Am I not your donkey, on which you have ridden all your life long until today? Was I ever in the habit of doing so to you?" He said, "No."

31 Then Yahweh opened the eyes of Balaam, and he saw Yahweh's angel standing in the way, with his sword drawn in his hand; and he bowed his head and fell on his face. **32** Yahweh's angel said to him, "Why have you struck your donkey <u>these three times</u>? Behold, I have come out as an adversary, because your way is perverse before me. **33** The donkey saw me and turned aside before me <u>these three times</u>. Unless she had turned aside from me, surely now I would have killed you, and saved her alive." **34** Balaam said to Yahweh's angel, "I have sinned; for I didn't know that you stood in the way against me. Now therefore, if it displeases you, I will go back again." **35** Yahweh's angel said to Balaam, "Go with the men; but you shall only speak the word that I shall speak to you." So Balaam went with the princes of Balak.

1Cor 12:4 Now there are **various kinds of gifts**, but the same Spirit.

5 There are **various kinds of service**, and the same Lord.

6 There are **various kinds of workings**, but the same God, **who works all things in all**.

NOTE: The three references by Paul in verses 4-6 of the "various kinds" of workings parallel the three times that the donkey "saw Yahweh's angel." But Paul must have seen something else, because the phrase "these three times" is itself spoken three times, in verses 28, 32, and 33. From this account, Paul must have derived that the work of God's spirit comes in nine "Gifts of the Spirit" which are commonly categorized into three groups of three! It is also interesting that "Yahweh's angel" appears ten times in the passage.

Num 22:36 When Balak heard that Balaam had come, he went out to meet him to the City of Moab, which is on the border of the Arnon, which is in the utmost part of the border. **37** Balak said to Balaam, "Didn't I earnestly send to you to call you? Why didn't you come to me? Am I not able indeed to promote you to honor?" **38 Balaam** said to Balak, "Behold, I have come to you. Have I now any power at all to speak anything? **The word that God puts in my mouth, that shall I speak**." **39** Balaam went with Balak, and they came to Kiriath Huzoth. **40** Balak sacrificed cattle and sheep, and sent to Balaam, **and to the princes who were with him**.

41 In the morning, Balak took Balaam, and brought him up into the high places of Baal; and he saw from there part of the people.

1Cor 12:7 But to each

one is given the **manifestation of the Spirit**

for the profit of all.

NOTE: Concerning the phrase "for the profit of all," the princes with Balak were also benefited to hear Balaam's words.

Numbers 23:1 – 24:25. First Pass

1 Cor. 12:8

Num 23:1 Balaam said to Balak, "Build here seven altars for me, and prepare here seven bulls and seven rams for me." **2** Balak did as Balaam had spoken; and Balak and Balaam offered on every altar a bull and a ram. **3** Balaam said to Balak, "Stand by your burnt offering, and I will go. Perhaps Yahweh will come to meet me. Whatever he shows me I will tell you." He went to a bare height.

EXCERPT FROM BALAAM'S FIRST BLESSING: 23:9-10.

9 For from the top of the rocks I see him, from the hills I see him. Behold, it is a people that dwells alone and shall not be listed among the nations. **10 Who can count the dust of Jacob, or count the fourth part of Israel**? Let me die the death of the righteous, and let my end be like his!"

EXCERPT FROM BALAAM'S SECOND BLESSING: 23:21-24.

21 He has not seen iniquity in Jacob. Neither has he seen perverseness in Israel. Yahweh his God is with him. The shout of a king is among them. **22 God brings them out of Egypt**. He has as it were the strength of the wild ox. **23** Surely there is no enchantment with Jacob; Neither is there any divination with Israel. Now it shall be said of Jacob and of Israel, what has God done! **24** Behold, a people rises up as a lioness. As a lion he lifts himself up. He shall not lie down until he eats of the prey and drinks the blood of the slain."

EXCERPT FROM BALAAM'S THIRD BLESSING: 24:4-8.

24:4 he says, who hears the words of God, who sees the vision of the Almighty, falling down, and having his eyes open: **5** How goodly are your tents, Jacob, and your dwellings, Israel! **6** As valleys they are spread out, as gardens by the riverside, as aloes which Yahweh has planted, as cedar trees beside the waters. **7 Water shall flow from his buckets. His seed shall be in many waters**. His king shall be higher than Agag. His kingdom shall be exalted. **8** God brings him out of Egypt. He has as it were the strength of the wild ox. He shall consume the nations his adversaries, shall break their bones in pieces, and pierce them with his arrows.

1Cor 12:8 For to one is given through the Spirit the word of wisdom, and to another the word of knowledge according to the same Spirit, **9** to another faith by the same Spirit,

and to another gifts of healings by the same Spirit, **10** and to another workings of miracles, and to another prophecy,

and to another discerning of spirits, to another different kinds of languages, and to another the interpretation of languages.

NOTE: The three blessings will be shown in their entirely later. Here, the nine gifts of the Spirit in 1 Corinthians 12:8-10 are echoed three at-a-time, in each of the first three blessings. (1) In 23:9 Israel is visibly set apart "from this hills I see him, a people that dwells alone" and is interpreted by Balaam with great wisdom. (2) Only a word of supernatural knowledge can possibly "count the dust" of Jacob. (3) Righteousness comes only by faith. (Gen 15:6). (4) Healing is linked to lack of iniquity and perverseness. (Ex. 15:26). (5) The Exodus was by miracles (Ex. 3:20). (6) Verse 23:24 is a well-known prophecy. (7) Eyes open to the spiritual world. (8) The sound of many languages spoken at once is referenced in Psalms, Isaiah and Revelation to be the sound of many waters. (Rev 19:6). (9) The final sentence of 24:8 builds upon the prophetic word in 23:24 but the words "*break* their bones" [*garam* in Heb.] and "*pierce them with his arrows*" [*machats* in Heb.] have their first Biblical mention in this verse.

The name of the Mesopotamian prophet **Balaam** [bil'am in Heb.] literally means "not of the people" in other words "foreigner."

1**Cor 24:11** But the one and the same Spirit produces all of these, distributing to each one separately as he desires.

12 For as the **body is one** and has many members, and all the members of the body, being many, are one body, so also is Christ. **13** For in one Spirit we were all baptized into one body, whether Jews or Greeks, whether bond or free; and were all given to drink into one Spirit.

14 For the body is not one member, but many. **15** If the foot would say, "Because I'm not the hand, I'm not part of the body," it is not therefore not part of the body. **16** If the ear would say, "Because I'm not the eye, I'm not part of the body," it's not therefore not part of the body. **17** If the whole body were an eye, where would the hearing be? If the whole were hearing, where would the smelling be? **18** But now God has set the members, each one of them, in the body, just as he desired. **19** If they were all one member, where would the body be? **20** But now they are many members, but one body. **21** The eye can't tell the hand, "I have no need for you," or again the head to the feet, "I have no need for you." **22** No, much rather, those members of the body which seem to be weaker are necessary. **23** Those parts of the body which we think to be less honorable, on these we bestow more abundant honor; and our unpresentable parts have more abundant modesty, **24** whereas our presentable parts have no such need. But God composed the body together, giving more abundant honor to the inferior part, **25** that there should be no division in the body, but that the members should have the same care for one another. **26** When one member suffers, all the members suffer with it. When one member is honored, all the members rejoice with it.

NOTE: In writing these next verses in 1 Corinthians 12:11-26 it seems that Paul is viewing Balaam as a single person, but seeing through that human person a picture of the body of Christ that is functioning in accordance to the workings of the one and same Spirit. Paul's verses here do not echo the details of Balaam's first three blessings, because he seems to be writing in view of Balaam as a concept. However, Paul has a plan. While he skips those details for now, he will soon return to the first three blessings of Balaam in their entirety and will interpret them from a completely different vantage point. That new vantage point has become one of the most treasured passages in the entire Bible.

Num 24:14 He said to Balak, "Come, I will let you know what this **people** will do to your people in the latter days." **15** He took up his parable, and said, "**Balaam the son of Beor** says, the man whose eyes are opened says; **16** he says, who hears the words of God, knows the knowledge of the Most High, and who sees the vision of the Almighty, falling down, and having his eyes open: **17** I see him, but not now. I see him, but not near. A star will come out of Jacob. A scepter will rise out of Israel, and shall strike through the corners of Moab, and crush all the sons of Sheth. **18** Edom shall be a possession. Seir, his enemy, also shall be a possession, while Israel does valiantly. **19** Out of Jacob shall one have dominion, and shall destroy the remnant from the city." **20** He looked at *Amalek*, and took up his parable, and said, "Amalek was the first of the nations, but his latter end shall come to destruction." **21** He looked at the Kenite, and took up his parable, and said, "Your dwelling place is strong. Your nest is set in the rock. **22** Nevertheless Kain shall be wasted, until Asshur carries you away captive." **23** He took up his parable, and said, "Alas, who shall live when God does this? **24** But ships shall come from the coast of Kittim. They shall afflict Asshur and shall afflict **Eber**. He also shall come to destruction."

1Cor 12:27 Now you are the

body of Christ,

and **members individually**.

28 God has set some in the assembly: first apostles, second prophets, third teachers, then *miracle* workers, then gifts of healings, helps, governments, and various kinds of **languages**.

29 Are all apostles? Are all prophets? Are all teachers? Are all miracle workers? **30** Do all have gifts of healings? Do all speak with various languages? Do all interpret?

NOTE: Paul now moves forward to address Balaam's famous prophecy, a prophecy for which Balak did not even ask. In Numbers 24:14-24 Paul calls out something that is entirely unexpected. In a passage about the destruction of eight different people groups, Paul gloriously sees the body of Christ in action, for the good of the whole world. (1) Apostles is connected to Moab whose leader, Balak, sent his leaders to bring in the prophet Balaam. (2) Prophets being connected by Paul to Sheth (Seth) might stem from the prophetic seed of Gen 3:15 and Gen 4:25. (3) Teachers is connected to Edom. (4) Miracles to Amalek. (5) Healings to the Kenites and its city Kain. (6) Helps to Asshur. (Assyria). (7) Kittim to governments (Cypress). (8) Eber to languages and their interpretation. In Jewish tradition a prophetic school was run by Shem and Eber in the time of the patriarchs.

Num 24:25 Balaam rose up and went and returned to his place; and Balak also went his **way**.

1Cor 12:31 But earnestly desire the best gifts. Moreover, I show a most excellent **way** to you.

NOTE: Up to this point, Paul seems to have ignored the sin of Balak, focusing only on the positive aspects of the story. But, in a dramatic phrase perhaps best described in NASB "And I show a still more excellent way" he revisits the first three blessings of Balaam and re-interprets them in light of what was lacking in Balak, and in so doing writes the famous chapter on love!

Numbers 23:1 – 24:25. Second Pass   1 Corinthians 13

Num 23:1 Balaam said to Balak, "Build here seven altars for me, and prepare here seven bulls and seven rams for me." **2** Balak did as Balaam had spoken; and Balak and Balaam offered on every altar a bull and a ram. **3** Balaam said to Balak, "Stand by your burnt offering, and I will go. Perhaps Yahweh will come to meet me. **Whatever he shows me I will tell you**." He went to a bare height.

4 God met Balaam, and he said to him, "I have prepared the seven altars, and I have offered up a bull and a ram on every altar." **5** Yahweh put a word in Balaam's mouth, and said, "Return to Balak, and thus you shall speak." **6** He returned to him, and behold, he was standing by his burnt offering, he, and all the princes of Moab. **7** He took up his parable, and said, "From Aram has Balak brought me, the king of Moab **from the mountains of the East**. Come, curse Jacob for me. Come, defy Israel.

8 How shall I curse whom God has not cursed? How shall I defy whom Yahweh has not defied? **9** For from the top of the rocks I see him, from the hills I see him. Behold, it is a people that dwells alone and shall not be listed among the nations. **10** Who can count the dust of Jacob, or count the **fourth part of Israel**? Let me **die the death of the righteous** and let my end be like his!"

11 Balak said to Balaam, "What have you done to me? I took you to curse my enemies, and behold, you have blessed them altogether." **23:12** He answered and said, "Must I not take heed to speak that which Yahweh puts in my mouth?"

1Cor 13:1 If I speak with the languages of men and of angels, but don't have love, I have become sounding brass or a clanging cymbal. **2** If I have the gift of prophecy, and know all mysteries and all knowledge, and if I **have all faith**, so as to remove **mountains**, but don't have love, I am nothing. **3** If I give away all my goods to **feed the poor**, and if I **give my body to be burned**, but don't have love, it profits me nothing.

NOTE: The first blessing of Balaam echoes the first section of 1 Corinthians 13. While speaking overall about love, Paul emphasizes *faith* that can remove mountains. Balak's faith was misplaced, being in Balaam rather than in God.

Num 23:13 Balak said to him, "Please come with me to another place, where you may see them. You shall see only part of them and shall not see them all. Curse them from there for me." **14** He took him into the field of Zophim, to the top of Pisgah, and built seven altars, and offered up a bull and a ram on every altar. **15** He said to Balak, "Stand here by your burnt offering, **while I meet Yahweh yonder**." **16** Yahweh met Balaam, and put a word in his mouth, and said, "Return to Balak, and say this." **17** He came to him, and behold, he was standing by his burnt offering, and the princes of Moab with him. Balak said to him, "What has Yahweh spoken?" **18** He took up his parable, and said,

"Rise up, Balak, and hear! Listen to me, you son of Zippor. **19** God is not a man, that he should lie, nor a son of man, that he should repent. Has he said, and will he not do it? **Or has he spoken, and will he not make it good**? **20** Behold, I have received a command to bless. He has blessed, and I can't reverse it. **21** He has not seen iniquity in Jacob. Neither has he seen perverseness in Israel. Yahweh his God is with him. The shout of a king is among them. **22** God brings them out of Egypt. He has as it were the strength of the wild ox. **23** Surely there is no enchantment with Jacob; Neither is there any divination with Israel. Now it shall be said of Jacob and of Israel, what has God done! **24** Behold, a people rises up as a lioness. As a lion he lifts himself up. He shall not lie down until he eats of the prey and drinks the blood of the slain."

1Cor 13:4 Love is patient and is kind. Love doesn't envy. Love doesn't brag, is not proud, **5** doesn't behave itself inappropriately, **doesn't seek its own way**, is not provoked, takes no account of evil; **6** doesn't rejoice in unrighteousness, but rejoices with the truth; **7** bears all things, believes all things, **hopes all things**, endures all things.

NOTE: The second blessing of Balaam echoes the second section of 1 Corinthians 13. While speaking overall about love, Paul emphasizes not faith but rather *hope*. Balak's hope was misplaced, and so he became disappointed in both Balaam and God.

Num 23:25 Balak said to Balaam, "Neither curse them at all, nor bless them at all." **26** But Balaam answered Balak, "Didn't I tell you, saying, '**All that Yahweh speaks, that I must do**'?"

27 Balak said to Balaam, "Come now, I will take you to another place; perhaps it will please God that you may curse them for me from there." **28** Balak took Balaam to the top of Peor, that looks down on the desert. **29** Balaam said to Balak, "Build seven altars for me here, and prepare seven bulls and seven rams for me here." **30** Balak did as Balaam had said, and offered up a bull and a ram on every altar.

Numbers 24

24:1 When Balaam saw that it pleased Yahweh to bless Israel, he didn't go, as at the other times, to use **divination**, but he set his face toward the wilderness. **2** Balaam lifted up his eyes, and he saw Israel dwelling according to their tribes; and the *Spirit of God came on him*.

3 He took up his parable, and said, "Balaam the son of Beor says, the man whose eyes are open says; **4** he says, who hears the words of God, **who sees the vision of the Almighty, falling down, and having his eyes open**: **5** How goodly are your tents, Jacob, and your dwellings, Israel! **6** As valleys they are spread out, as gardens by the riverside, as aloes which Yahweh has planted, as cedar trees beside the waters. **7** Water shall flow from his buckets. His seed shall be in many waters. His king shall be higher than Agag. His kingdom shall be exalted. **8** God brings him out of Egypt. He has as it were the strength of the wild ox. He shall consume the nations his adversaries, shall break their bones in pieces, and pierce them with his arrows. **9** He couched, he lay down as a lion, as a lioness; who shall rouse him up? Everyone who blesses you is blessed. Everyone who curses you is cursed."

1Cor 13:8

Love never fails. But where there are prophecies, they will be done away with. Where there are various languages, they will cease. Where there is **knowledge**, it will be done away with. **9** For we know in part, and we prophesy in part; **10** but *when that which is complete has come*, then that which is partial will be done away with. **11** When I was a child, I spoke as a child, I felt as a child, I thought as a child. Now that I have become a man, I have put away childish things. **12** **For now we see in a mirror, dimly, but then face to face**. Now I know in part, but then I will know fully, even as I was also fully known.

NOTE: The third blessing of Balaam echoes the third section of 1 Corinthians 13. Balak completely failed in his endeavor because his motivation and actions did not stem from love.

Num 24:10 Balak's anger burned against Balaam, and he struck his hands together. Balak said to Balaam, "I called you to curse my enemies, and behold, you have altogether blessed them **these three times**. **11** Therefore now flee to your place! I thought to promote you to great honor; but, behold, Yahweh has kept you back from honor." **12** Balaam said to Balak, "Didn't I also tell your messengers whom you sent to me, saying, **13** 'If Balak would give me his house full of silver and gold, I can't go beyond the word of Yahweh, to do either good or bad from my own mind. I will say what Yahweh says'?"

1Cor 13:13 But now faith, hope, and love remain—

these three. The greatest of these is love.

NOTE: Paul summarizes his tribute to love even as Balak summarizes his anger towards Balaam.

Numbers 24:14	1 Corinthians 14

Num 24:14 He said to Balak, "**Come,**

I will let you know what this people will do to your people in the latter days."

15 He took up his **parable**, and said, "Balaam the son of Beor says, **the man whose eyes are opened says: 16 he says, who hears the words of God, knows the knowledge of the Most High, and who sees the vision of the Almighty, falling down, and having his eyes open**: 17 I see him, but not now. I see him, but not near. *A star will come out of Jacob. A scepter will rise out of Israel,* and shall strike through the corners of Moab, and crush all the sons of **Sheth**. 18 Edom shall be a possession. Seir, his enemy, also shall be a possession, while Israel does valiantly. **19** Out of Jacob shall one have dominion, and shall destroy the remnant from the city." **20** He looked at Amalek, and took up his parable, and said, "Amalek was the first of the nations, but his latter end shall come to destruction." **21** He looked at the Kenite, and took up his parable, and said, "Your dwelling place is strong. Your nest is set in the rock. **22** Nevertheless Kain shall be wasted, until Asshur carries you away captive." **23** He took up his parable, and said, "Alas, who shall live when God does this? **24** But ships shall come from the coast of Kittim. They shall afflict Asshur and shall afflict **Eber**. He also shall come to destruction."

25 Balaam rose up and went and returned to his place; and Balak also went his way.

1Cor 14:1 Follow after love and earnestly desire spiritual gifts, but **especially that you may prophesy**. 2 For he who speaks in another language speaks not to men, but to God; **for no one understands**, but **in the Spirit he speaks mysteries**. 3 But he who *prophesies speaks to men for their edification, exhortation, and consolation*. 4 He who speaks in another language edifies himself, but he who **prophesies** edifies the assembly. **5** Now I desire to have you all speak with other languages, but rather that you would prophesy. For he is greater who prophesies than he who speaks with other **languages**, unless he interprets, that the assembly may be built up.

NOTE: The phrase "a star will come out of Jacob" has been widely interpreted as the famous prophetic word that brought the wise men to Jesus' birth. Indeed, that prophetic word from Balaam did not go unheeded! The echo of prophecies to Sheth (Seth) and languages to Eber is based on the prior echoes described in 1 Corinthians 12:27-28.

Numbers 25

1 Corinthians 14:6

Num 25:1 Israel stayed in Shittim; and the people began to play the prostitute with the daughters of Moab. **2** For they called the people to the sacrifices of their gods. The people ate and bowed down to their gods. **3** Israel joined himself to Baal Peor, and Yahweh's anger burned against Israel. **4** Yahweh said to Moses, "Take all the chiefs of the people, and hang them up to Yahweh before the sun, that the fierce anger of Yahweh may turn away from Israel." **5** Moses said to the judges of Israel, "Everyone kill his men who have joined themselves to Baal Peor."

6 Behold, one of the children of Israel came and brought to his **brothers** a Midianite woman in the sight of Moses, and in the sight of all the congregation of the children of Israel, while they were weeping at the door of the Tent of Meeting. **7** When Phinehas, the son of Eleazar, the son of Aaron the priest, saw it, **he rose up from the middle of the congregation**, and took a spear in his hand. **8 He went after the man of Israel into the pavilion, and thrust both of them through**, the man of Israel, and the woman through her body. So, **the plague was stopped among the children of Israel**. **9** Those who died by the plague were twenty-four thousand.

1Cor 14:6 But now, **brothers**, if I come to you **speaking with other languages**, what would I profit you, unless I speak to you either by way of revelation, or of knowledge, or of prophesying, or of teaching? **7** Even things without life, giving a voice, whether pipe or harp, if they didn't give a distinction in the sounds, how would it be known what is piped or harped? **8** For if the trumpet gave an uncertain sound, who would prepare himself for war? **9** So also you, unless you uttered by the tongue words easy to understand, how would it be known what is spoken? For you would be speaking into the air. **10** There are, it may be, so many kinds of languages in the world, and none of them is without meaning. **11** If then I don't know the meaning of the language, I would be to him who speaks a foreigner, and he who speaks would be a foreigner to me. **12** So also you, **since you are zealous** for spiritual gifts, seek that you may abound **to the building up of the assembly**.

NOTE: [Balak ends.] What Phinehas did was from God, but his actions were not understood by the people until God "interpreted them" for the people in the next section. See the next section for details.

Numbers 25:10	1 Corinthians 14:13

Num 25:10 Yahweh spoke to Moses, saying, **11** "**Phinehas**, the son of Eleazar, the son of Aaron the priest, **has turned my wrath away** from the children of Israel, in that he was jealous with my jealousy among them, so that **I didn't consume the children of Israel** in my jealousy. **12** Therefore say, '**Behold, I give to him my covenant of peace**. **13** It shall be to him, and to his offspring after him, the covenant of an everlasting priesthood, because he was jealous for his God, and made atonement for the children of Israel.'"

1Cor 14:13 Therefore let **him who speaks in another language** pray that he may interpret. **14** For if I **pray in another language**, my spirit prays, but my understanding is unfruitful. **15** What is it then? I will pray with the spirit, and I will pray with the understanding also. I will sing with the spirit, and I will sing with the understanding also. **16** Otherwise if you **bless with the spirit**, how will he who fills the place of the unlearned say the "Amen" at your giving of thanks, seeing he doesn't know what you say? **17** For you most certainly give thanks well, but the other person is not built up. **18** I thank my God, I speak with other languages more than you all. **19** However, in the assembly I would rather **speak five words** with my understanding that I might instruct others also, than ten thousand words in another language.

NOTE: [Pinchas.] Phinehas means "mouth of a serpent." But it seems Paul is essentially saying that the actions he took in view of the whole assembly of Israel were actions that were not understood, and so metaphorically he was "speaking in another language."

NOTE: The echo of "five words" to Numbers 25:12 is fascinating. The phrase "Behold, I give to him my covenant of peace" is recorded in five Hebrew words. (1) Behold = hineh. (2) I give = natan. (3) to him = lo. (4) My covenant = berith. (5) of peace = shalom.

7965 [e]	1285 [e]	853 [e]		5414 [e]	2005 [e]	559 [e]	3651 [e]
šā·lō·wm.	bə·rî·ṯî	'eṯ-	lōw	nō·ṯên	hin·nî	'ê·mōr;	lā·ḵên
שָׁלוֹם: —	בְּרִיתִי	אֶת־	לֹו	נֹתֵן	הִנְנִי ,	אֱמֹר	לָכֵן 12
of peace	My covenant	-	to him	I give	behold	say	Therefore
N-ms	N-fsc | 1cs	DirObjM	Prep | 3ms	V-Qal-Prtcpl-ms	Interjection | 1cs	V-Qal-imp-ms	Adv

Source: BibleHub.com

(Alternatively, If one considers the Aleph-Tav (et) as its own written word even though not pronounced, then the body of the phrase: "I give to him my covenant of peace" comprises exactly five Hebrew words.)

Num 25:14 Now the name of the **man of Israel** that was slain, who was slain with the Midianite woman, was Zimri, the son of Salu, a prince of a fathers' house among the Simeonites. **15** The name of the Midianite woman who was slain was Cozbi, the daughter of Zur. He was head of the people of a fathers' house in Midian.

16 Yahweh spoke to Moses, saying, **17** "**Harass the Midianites, and strike them**; **18** for **they harassed you with their wiles, wherein they have deceived you** in the matter of Peor, and in the matter of Cozbi, the daughter of the prince of Midian, their sister, who was slain on the day of the plague in the matter of Peor."

1Cor 14:20 Brothers, don't be children in mind, but be babies in malice, and in mind be men. **21** In the law it is written, "By men of strange languages and by the lips of strangers I will speak to this people. Not even thus will they hear me, says the Lord." **22** Therefore other languages are for a sign, not to those who believe, but to the unbelieving; but prophesying is for a sign, not to the unbelieving, but to those who believe. **23** If therefore the whole assembly is assembled together and all speak with other languages, and unlearned or unbelieving people come in, won't they say that you are crazy? **24** But if all prophesy, and someone unbelieving or unlearned comes in, he is **reproved** by all, and he is **judged by all**. **25** And thus the secrets of his heart are revealed. So he will fall down on his face and worship God, declaring that God is among you indeed.

NOTE: This echo is mostly conceptual as a whole, rather than with individual elements. Paul's the whole assembly echoes Israel; men who speaks in strange languages: Phineas; the unlearned: Zimri, son of Salu of the Simeonites; the unbelieving Cozbi, daughter of the prince of Midian. Apparently, Paul is implying that Phineas' uninterpreted actions toward Zimri and Cozbi were understood better by the Midianites than by the Israelites, while God's clear prophetic explanation through Moses was better understood by the people of Israel than the Midianites (1 Cor. 14:21-22). Cozbi might have been ordered by her father to seduce Zimri, but Zimri, while part of the assembly of Israel, should have known better (v23), and needed instruction. Paul's concluding words, "he will fall down on his face and worship God," may have been chosen as a potential echo to the Peor situation as well.

Numbers 26	1 Corinthians 14:26

Num 26:1 After the plague, Yahweh spoke to Moses and to Eleazar the son of Aaron the priest, saying, **2** "**Take a census of all the congregation** of the children of Israel, from twenty years old and upward, by their fathers' houses, **all who are able to go out to war** in Israel." **3** Moses and Eleazar the priest spoke with them in the plains of Moab by the Jordan at Jericho, saying, **4** "[Take a census of the people], from twenty years old and **upward, as Yahweh commanded Moses and the children of Israel." These are those that came out** of the land of Egypt.

1Cor 14:26 What is it then, brothers? **When you come together, each one of you has a psalm, has a teaching, has a revelation, has another language, or has an interpretation**.

Let all things be done to build each other up.

Num 26:5 Reuben, the firstborn of Israel; the sons of Reuben: of Hanoch, the family of the Hanochites; of Pallu, the family of the Palluites; **6** of Hezron, the family of the Hezronites; of Carmi, the family of the Carmites. **7** These are the families of the Reubenites; and those who were counted of them were forty-three thousand seven hundred thirty. **8** The sons of Pallu: Eliab. **9** The sons of Eliab: **Nemuel, Dathan, and Abiram. These are that Dathan and Abiram who were called by the congregation**, who strove against Moses and against Aaron in the company of Korah when they strove against Yahweh; **10** and the earth opened its mouth, and swallowed them up together with Korah when that company died; when the fire devoured two hundred fifty men, **and they became a sign**. **11** Notwithstanding, the sons of Korah didn't die.

12 The sons of Simeon after their families: of Nemuel, the family of the Nemuelites; of Jamin, the family of the Jaminites; of Jachin, the family of the Jachinites; **13** of Zerah, the family of the Zerahites; of Shaul, the family of the Shaulites. **14** These are the families of the Simeonites, twenty-two thousand two hundred.

15 The sons of Gad after their families: of Zephon, the family of the Zephonites; of Haggi, the family of the Haggites; of Shuni, the family of the Shunites; **16** of Ozni, the family of the Oznites; of Eri, the family of the Erites; **17** of Arod, the family of the Arodites; of Areli, the family of the Arelites. **18** These are the families of the sons of Gad according to those who were counted of them, forty thousand five hundred.

1Cor 14:27 If any man speaks in another language, **let there be two, or at the most three**, and in turn; and let one interpret. **28** But if there is no interpreter, **let him keep silent in the assembly, and let him speak to himself and to God**.

NOTE: Concerning the second proposed echo between 1 Corinthians 14:28 and Numbers 26:10: Numbers 16:25-27 implies that Dathan and Abiram were silent as they stood at the doorway of their tents waiting for God's judgement about their prior statements against Moses motivations. If this echo is intentional, then Paul is implicitly saying that a word spoken in an unknown language, but not interpreted in the assembly, by its very lack of interpretation, is itself a "sign" to the assembly.

Num 26:19 The sons of Judah: Er and Onan. Er and Onan died in the land of Canaan. **20** The sons of Judah after their families were: of **Shelah**, the family of the Shelanites; of **Perez**, the family of the Perezites; of **Zerah**, the family of the Zerahites. **21** The sons of Perez were: of Hezron, the family of the Hezronites; of Hamul, the family of the Hamulites. **22** These are the families of Judah according to those who were counted of them, seventy-six thousand five hundred.

23 The sons of Issachar after their families: of Tola, the family of the Tolaites; of Puvah, the family of the Punites; **24** of Jashub, the family of the Jashubites; of Shimron, the family of the Shimronites. **25** These are the families of Issachar according to those who were counted of them, sixty-four thousand three hundred.

26 The sons of Zebulun after their families: of Sered, the family of the Seredites; of Elon, the family of the Elonites; of Jahleel, the family of the Jahleelites. **27** These are the families of the Zebulunites according to those who were counted of them, sixty thousand five hundred.

28 The sons of Joseph after their families: Manasseh and Ephraim.

1Cor 14:29

Let the **prophets speak, two or three**, and let the others discern.

NOTE: Perez and Zerah's births were famously prophetic. Of their brother Shelah, less is written, nevertheless three brother are listed, echoing Paul's words: "two or three."

Num 26:29 The sons of Manasseh: of Machir, the family of the Machirites; and Machir became the father of Gilead; of Gilead, the family of the Gileadites. **30** These are the sons of Gilead: of Iezer, the family of the Iezerites; of Helek, the family of the Helekites; **31** and of Asriel, the family of the Asrielites; and of Shechem, the family of the Shechemites; **32** and of Shemida, the family of the Shemidaites; and of Hepher, the family of the Hepherites. **33** Zelophehad the son of Hepher had no sons, but daughters: and the names of the **daughters of Zelophehad** were **Mahlah, Noah, Hoglah, Milcah, and Tirzah**. **34** These are the families of Manasseh. Those who were counted of them were fifty-two thousand seven hundred.

35 These are the sons of Ephraim after their families: of Shuthelah, the family of the Shuthelahites; of Becher, the family of the Becherites; of Tahan, the family of the Tahanites. **36** These are the sons of Shuthelah: of Eran, the family of the Eranites. **37** These are the families of the sons of Ephraim according to those who were counted of them, thirty-two thousand five hundred. These are the sons of Joseph after their families.

1Cor 14:30 But if a **revelation is made to another sitting by**, let the first keep silent. **31** For you **all can prophesy one by one**, that all may learn, and all may be exhorted.

NOTE: Concerning the proposed echo of "revelation" to the "daughters of Zelophehad, Paul's already said in 14:29 that "when you come together each one" has something to offer. This must include women. And while Paul speaks to gender in 14:34, here in 14:30-31 he speaks from principle without mentioning gender. Yet his echo apparently alludes to the *revelation* that must have preceded the daughters of Zelophehad's *appearance* before Moses! Indeed, that account in Numbers did result in both learning and exhortation of all Israel, as their *revelation* became accepted as part of the commandments of God towards Israel.

Num 26:38 The sons of Benjamin after their family: of Bela, the family of the Belaites; of Ashbel, the family of the Ashbelites; of Ahiram, the family of the Ahiramites; **39** of Shephupham, the family of the Shuphamites; of Hupham, the family of the Huphamites. **40** The sons of Bela were Ard and Naaman: [of Ard], the family of the Ardites; of Naaman, the family of the Naamites. **41** These are the sons of Benjamin after their families; and those who were counted of them were forty-five thousand six hundred.

42 These are the sons of Dan after their families: of Shuham, the family of the Shuhamites. These are the families of Dan after their families. **43** All the families of the Shuhamites, according to those who were counted of them, were sixty-four thousand four hundred. **44** The sons of Asher after their families: of Imnah, the family of the Imnites; of Ishvi, the family of the Ishvites; of Beriah, the family of the Berites. **45** Of the sons of Beriah: of Heber, the family of the Heberites; of Malchiel, the family of the Malchielites. **46** The name of the daughter of Asher was Serah. **47** These are the families of the sons of Asher according to those who were counted of them, fifty-three thousand and four hundred.

48 The sons of Naphtali after their families: of Jahzeel, the family of the Jahzeelites; of Guni, the family of the Gunites; **49** of Jezer, the family of the Jezerites; of Shillem, the family of the Shillemites. **50** These are the families of Naphtali according to their families; and those who were counted of them were forty-five thousand four hundred.

NOTE: These verses seem to be skipped by Paul.

Num 26:51 These are those who were counted of the children of Israel, six hundred one thousand seven hundred thirty.

52 Yahweh spoke to Moses, saying, **53** "To these the land shall be divided for an inheritance according to the number of names. **54** To the more you shall give the more inheritance, and to the fewer you shall give the less inheritance. **To everyone according to those who were counted of him shall his inheritance be given**. **55** Notwithstanding, the land shall be divided by lot. According to the names of the tribes of their fathers they shall inherit. **56** According to the lot shall their inheritance be divided between the more and the fewer."

1Cor 14:32 The **spirits of the prophets are subject** to the prophets,

NOTE: Each person in Israel carried responsibility to work within the boundaries of the *land* God gives to them. Each prophet carries responsibility for staying within the boundaries of the *prophetic gift* that God gives to them. Does Paul perhaps see the prophetic gifts to the assembly as in some way having "positional assignments" in the kingdom of God?

Num 26:57 These are those who were counted of the Levites after their families: of Gershon, the family of the Gershonites; of Kohath, the family of the Kohathites; of Merari, the family of the Merarites. **58** These are the families of Levi: the family of the Libnites, the family of the Hebronites, the family of the Mahlites, the family of the Mushites, the family of the Korahites. Kohath became the father of Amram. **59** The name of Amram's wife was Jochebed, the daughter of Levi, who was born to Levi in Egypt. She bore to Amram Aaron and Moses, and Miriam their sister. **60** To Aaron were born Nadab and Abihu, Eleazar and Ithamar. **61** Nadab and Abihu died **when they offered strange fire before Yahweh**. **62** Those who were counted of them were twenty-three thousand, every male from a month old and upward; for they were not counted among the children of Israel, because there was no inheritance given them among the children of Israel.

63 These are those who were counted by Moses and Eleazar the priest, who counted the children of Israel in the plains of Moab by the Jordan at Jericho. **64 But among these there was not a man of them who were counted by Moses and Aaron the priest, who counted the children of Israel in the wilderness of Sinai**. **65** For Yahweh had said of them, "They shall surely die in the wilderness." There was not a man left of them, except Caleb the son of Jephunneh, and Joshua the son of Nun.

1Cor 14:33 for **God is not a God of confusion**, but of **peace**, as in all the assemblies of the saints.

NOTE: Numbers 26:64 is proposed to be the echo of "peace" since the census was performed fully, properly, and completely. When a large difficult task is performed well, peace is the result. The final words of 1 Corinthians 14:33, "in all assemblies of the saints" may well imply all the assemblies everywhere, echoing the *entire list of tribes* in Numbers Ch. 26.

Numbers 27   1 Corinthians 14:34

Num 27:1 Then the **daughters** of Zelophehad, the son of Hepher, the son of Gilead, the son of Machir, the son of Manasseh, of the families of Manasseh the son of Joseph, came near. These are the names of his daughters: Mahlah, Noah, Hoglah, Milcah, and Tirzah. **2** They stood before Moses, before Eleazar the priest, and before the princes and all the congregation, at the door of the Tent of Meeting, <u>saying</u>, **3** "Our father died in the wilderness. He was not among the company of those who gathered themselves together against Yahweh in the company of Korah, but he died in his own sin. He had no sons. **4** Why should the name of our father be taken away from among his family, because he had no son? Give us a possession among the brothers of our father." **27:5 Moses brought their cause before Yahweh**.

6 Yahweh spoke to Moses, saying, **7** "The daughters of Zelophehad speak right. You shall surely give them a possession of an inheritance among their father's brothers. You shall cause the inheritance of their father to pass to them. **8** You shall speak to the children of Israel, saying, 'If a man dies, and has no son, then you shall cause his inheritance to pass to his daughter. **9** If he has no daughter, then you shall give his inheritance to his brothers. **10** If he has no brothers, then you shall give his inheritance to his father's brothers. **11** If his father has no brothers, then you shall give his inheritance to his kinsman who is next to him of his family, and he shall possess it. This shall be a statute and ordinance for the **children of Israel**, as Yahweh commanded Moses.'"

1Cor 14:34 Let your **wives [women]** keep silent in the assemblies, for it has not been permitted for them to **speak**;

but **let them be in subjection**, as the law also says.

35 If they desire to learn anything, let them ask their own husbands at home, for it is shameful for a woman to chatter in the **assembly**.

NOTE: This is one of the most difficult of Paul's passages to explain. Many Christian theologians, looking at the New Testament as a whole have deduced that Paul's meaning of "keep silent" should not be taken literally. This echo supports that view: the daughters *did* speak, and moreover when they spoke they *stood before the entire congregation*! However, in their speaking they did not raise themselves above the leadership. In this account they did not demand change on the basis of having heard God but rather spoke to a situation and asked an important challenging question, and proposed a solution. They gave Moses time to take the matter to God, and time for God to speak to Moses (i.e. the leadership). God spoke to Moses and said the women "speak right" (Numbers 27:7).

Num 27:12 Yahweh said to **Moses, "Go up into this mountain** of Abarim, and see the land which I have given to the children of Israel. **13** When you have seen it, <u>you also shall be gathered to your people</u>, as **Aaron your brother** was gathered; **14** because you rebelled against my word in the wilderness of Zin, in the strife of the congregation, to sanctify me at the waters before their eyes." (These are the waters of Meribah of Kadesh in the wilderness of Zin.)

1Cor 14:36 What?

Was it from you that

the <u>word of God went out</u>?

Or did it **come to you alone**?

NOTE: In this concluding verse regarding women, Paul challenges women as to whether it was through them that the word of God went out. Indeed, these verses echo the thought that yes, it was from Moses that the entire Torah did "go out" to Israel and beyond. But, while Paul's questions may read as a bit harsh to women, the echoed passage should strike a "fear of the Lord" to men, for in these echoed verses, both Moses and Aaron are being judged for their prior handling the received Word of God. Paul's heart seems to be full and clear here. Yes, the word of God went out through men, but if men abuse that privilege, God can and will judge them directly for any misuse of that positional authority before God! It is in that context that Paul challenges women!

Num 27:15 **Moses spoke to Yahweh, saying, 16** "<u>Let Yahweh, the God of the spirits of all flesh, appoint a man over the congregation, 17 who may go out before them, and who may come in before them, and who may lead them out, and who may bring them in, that the congregation of Yahweh may not be as sheep which have no shepherd.</u>" **18** Yahweh said to Moses, "Take Joshua the son of Nun, a man in whom is the Spirit, and lay your hand on him. **19** Set him before Eleazar the priest, and before all the congregation; and commission him in their sight. **20** You shall give authority to him, **that all the congregation of the children of Israel may obey**. **21** He shall stand before Eleazar the priest, <u>who shall inquire for him by the judgment of the Urim before Yahweh</u>. At his word they shall go out, and at his word they shall come in, **both he and all the children of Israel with him**, even all the congregation." **22** Moses did as Yahweh commanded him; and he took Joshua, and set him before Eleazar the priest and before all the congregation. **23** He laid his hands on him and commissioned him, as Yahweh spoke by Moses.

1Cor 14:37 **If any man thinks himself to be a prophet or spiritual**, let him recognize the things which <u>I write to you, that they are the commandment of the Lord</u>. 38 But **if anyone is ignorant, let him be ignorant**.

39 Therefore, brothers, <u>desire earnestly to prophesy</u>, and don't forbid **speaking with other languages**.

NOTE: Numbers 27:15 is unique in the rendering that this time it was "Moses spoke to Yahweh, saying." Moses then tells Yahweh that he, God, should appoint a man over the congregation. In 1 Corinthians 14:37, Paul's sentence is similarly bold! He tells the Corinthians that the things "I write to you" are "the commandment of the Lord." Paul's word "Lord" might specifically echo Moses's word "shepherd," a phrase which Jesus himself quotes in Matthew 9:36.

Numbers 28   ## 1 Corinthians 14:40

Num 28:1 Yahweh spoke to Moses, saying, **2** "Command the children of Israel, and tell them, 'See that you present my offering, my food for my offerings made by fire, of a pleasant aroma to me, in their due season.' **3** You shall tell them, 'This is the offering made by fire which you shall offer to Yahweh: male lambs a year old without defect, two day by day, for a continual burnt offering. **4** You shall offer the one lamb in the morning, and you shall offer the other lamb at evening, **5** with one tenth of an ephah of fine flour for a meal offering, mixed with the fourth part of a hin of beaten oil. **6** It is a continual burnt offering which was ordained in Mount Sinai for a pleasant aroma, an offering made by fire to Yahweh. **7** Its drink offering shall be the fourth part of a hin for each lamb. You shall pour out a drink offering of strong drink to Yahweh in the holy place. **8** The other lamb you shall offer at evening. As the meal offering of the morning, and as its drink offering, you shall offer it, an offering made by fire, for a pleasant aroma to Yahweh.

1Cor 14:40 Let all things be done decently and in order.

Num 28:9 "'On the Sabbath day, you shall offer two male lambs a year old without defect, and two tenths of an ephah of fine flour for a meal offering mixed with oil, and its drink offering: **10** this is the burnt offering of every Sabbath, besides the continual burnt offering and its drink offering.

1Cor 14:40 Let all things be done decently and in order.

(repeated)

NOTE: Paul, nearing the end of his primary purpose in writing 1 Corinthians, does not spend time developing thoughts about the feasts for this church. Instead, he speak at a high level about the importance "doing all things" and the manner of doing them. (See Leviticus/Romans for details of how Paul echoes Leviticus Ch. 23 regarding the feasts of the Lord.)

Num 28:11 "'In the beginnings of your months, you shall offer a burnt offering to Yahweh: two young bulls, one ram, seven male lambs a year old without defect, **12** and three tenths of an ephah of fine flour for a meal offering mixed with oil, for each bull; and two tenth parts of fine flour for a meal offering mixed with oil, for the one ram; **13** and one tenth part of fine flour mixed with oil for a meal offering to every lamb, for a burnt offering of a pleasant aroma, an offering made by fire to Yahweh. **14** Their drink offerings shall be half a hin of wine for a bull, the third part of a hin for the ram, and the fourth part of a hin for a lamb. This is the burnt offering of every month throughout the months of the year. **15** One male goat for a sin offering to Yahweh shall be offered, besides the continual burnt offering and its drink offering.

1Cor 14:40 Let all things be done decently and in order.

(repeated)

Num 28:16 "'In the first month, on the fourteenth day of the month, is Yahweh's Passover. **17** On the fifteenth day of this month shall be a feast. Unleavened bread shall be eaten for seven days. **18** In the first day shall be a holy convocation. You shall do no regular work, **19** but you shall offer an offering made by fire, a burnt offering to Yahweh: two young bulls, one ram, and seven male lambs a year old. They shall be to you without defect, **20** and their meal offering, fine flour mixed with oil. You shall offer three tenths for a bull, and two tenths for the ram. **21** You shall offer one tenth for every lamb of the seven lambs; **22** and one male goat for a sin offering, to make atonement for you. **23** You shall offer these besides the burnt offering of the morning, which is for a continual burnt offering. **24** In this way you shall offer daily, for seven days, the food of the offering made by fire, of a pleasant aroma to Yahweh. It shall be offered besides the continual burnt offering and its drink offering. **28:25** On the seventh day you shall have a holy convocation. You shall do no regular work.

1Cor 14:40 Let all things be done decently and in order.

(repeated)

Num 28:26 "'Also in the day of the first fruits, when you offer a new meal offering to Yahweh in your [feast of weeks], you shall have a holy convocation. You shall do no regular work. **27** You shall offer a burnt offering for a pleasant aroma to Yahweh: two young bulls, one ram, seven male lambs a year old; **28** and their meal offering, fine flour mixed with oil, three tenths for each bull, two tenths for the one ram, **29** one tenth for every lamb of the seven lambs; **30** one male goat, to make atonement for you. **31** Besides the continual burnt offering and its meal offering, you shall offer them and their drink offerings. See that they are without defect.'"

1Cor 14:40 Let all things be done decently and in order.

(repeated)

Numbers 29

1 Cor. 14:40

Num 29:1 "'In the seventh month, on the first day of the month, you shall have a holy convocation; you shall do no regular work. It is a day of blowing of trumpets to you. **2** You shall offer a burnt offering for a pleasant aroma to Yahweh: one young bull, one ram, seven male lambs a year old without defect; **3** and their meal offering, fine flour mixed with oil, three tenths for the bull, two tenths for the ram, **4** and one tenth for every lamb of the seven lambs; **5** and one male goat for a sin offering, to make atonement for you; **6** besides the burnt offering of the new moon, and its meal offering, and the continual burnt offering and its meal offering, and their drink offerings, according to their ordinance, for a pleasant aroma, an offering made by fire to Yahweh.

1Cor 14:40 Let all things be done decently and in order.

(repeated)

Num 29:7 "'On the tenth day of this seventh month you shall have a holy convocation. You shall afflict your souls. You shall do no kind of work; **8** but you shall offer a burnt offering to Yahweh for a pleasant aroma: one young bull, one ram, seven male lambs a year old, having no defect; **9** and their meal offering, fine flour mixed with oil, three tenths for the bull, two tenths for the one ram, **10** one tenth for every lamb of the seven lambs: **11** one male goat for a sin offering, besides the sin offering of atonement, and the continual burnt offering, and its meal offering, and their drink offerings.

1Cor 14:40 Let all things be done decently and in order.

(repeated)

Num 29:12 "'On the fifteenth day of the seventh month you shall have a holy convocation. You shall do no regular work. You shall keep a feast to Yahweh seven days. **13** You shall offer a burnt offering, an offering made by fire, of a pleasant aroma to Yahweh: thirteen young bulls, two rams, fourteen male lambs a year old, having no defect; **14** and their meal offering, fine flour mixed with oil, three tenths for every bull of the thirteen bulls, two tenths for each ram of the two rams, **15** and one tenth for every lamb of the fourteen lambs; **16** and one male goat for a sin offering, besides the continual burnt offering, its meal offering, and its drink offering.

1Cor 14:40 Let all things be done decently and in order.

(repeated)

Num 29:17 "'On the second day you shall offer twelve young bulls, two rams, fourteen male lambs a year old without defect; **18** and their meal offering and their drink offerings for the bulls, for the rams, and for the lambs, according to their number, after the ordinance; **19** and one male goat for a sin offering, besides the continual burnt offering, and its meal offering, and their drink offerings.

20 "'On the third day: eleven bulls, two rams, fourteen male lambs a year old without defect; **21** and their meal offering and their drink offerings for the bulls, for the rams, and for the lambs, according to their number, after the ordinance; **22** and one male goat for a sin offering, besides the continual burnt offering, and its meal offering, and its drink offering.

23 "'On the fourth day: ten bulls, two rams, fourteen male lambs a year old without defect; **24** their meal offering and their drink offerings for the bulls, for the rams, and for the lambs, according to their number, after the ordinance; **25** and one male goat for a sin offering; besides the continual burnt offering, its meal offering, and its drink offering.

29:26 "'On the fifth day: nine bulls, two rams, fourteen male lambs a year old without defect; **27** and their meal offering and their drink offerings for the bulls, for the rams, and for the lambs, according to their number, after the ordinance; **28** and one male goat for a sin offering, besides the continual burnt offering, and its meal offering, and its drink offering.

29 "'On the sixth day: eight bulls, two rams, fourteen male lambs a year old without defect; **30** and their meal offering and their drink offerings for the bulls, for the rams, and for the lambs, according to their number, after the ordinance; **31** and one male goat for a sin offering; besides the continual burnt offering, its meal offering, and its drink offerings.

32 "'On the seventh day: seven bulls, two rams, fourteen male lambs a year old without defect; **33** and their meal offering and their drink offerings for the bulls, for the rams, and for the lambs, according to their number, after the ordinance; **34** and one male goat for a sin offering; besides the continual burnt offering, its meal offering, and its drink offering.

35 "'On the eighth day you shall have a solemn assembly. You shall do no regular work; **36** but you shall offer a burnt offering, an offering made by fire, a pleasant aroma to Yahweh: one bull, one ram, seven male lambs a year old without defect; **37** their meal offering and their drink offerings for the bull, for the ram, and for the lambs, shall be according to their number, after the ordinance; **38** and one male goat for a sin offering, besides the continual burnt offering, and its meal offering, and its drink offering.

1Cor 14:40 Let all things be done decently and in order.

(repeated)

Num 29:39 "'You shall offer these to Yahweh in your set feasts—in addition to your vows and your free will offerings—for your burnt offerings, your meal offerings, your drink offerings, and your peace offerings.'" **40** Moses told the children of Israel according to all that Yahweh commanded Moses.

1Cor 14:40 Let all things be done decently and in order.

(repeated)

NOTE: [Pinchas ends.] However one decides to interpret Paul's use of the words "all things" readers would do well to place the emphasis on the words "decently" and "in order." That is to say, whatever an individual or assembly decides to "be done" regarding feasts should be done decently and orderly.

Numbers 30   1 Cor. 14:40

Num 30:1 Moses spoke to the heads of the tribes of the children of Israel, saying, "This is the thing which Yahweh has commanded. **2** When a man vows a vow to Yahweh or swears an oath to bind his soul with a bond, he shall not break his word. **He shall do according to all that proceeds out of his mouth**.

3 "Also, when a woman vows a vow to Yahweh and binds herself by a bond, being in her father's house, in her youth, **4** and her father hears her vow and her bond with which she has bound her soul, and her father says nothing to her, then all her vows shall stand, and every bond with which she has bound her soul shall stand. **5** But if her father forbids her in the day that he hears, none of her vows or of her bonds with which she has bound her soul shall stand. Yahweh will forgive her, because her father has forbidden her.

6 "If she has a husband, while her vows are on her, or the rash utterance of her lips with which she has bound her soul, **7** and her husband hears it, and says nothing to her in the day that he hears it; then her vows shall stand, and her bonds with which she has bound her soul shall stand. **8** But if her husband forbids her in the day that he hears it, then **he makes void her vow which is on her and the rash utterance of her lips**, with which she has bound her soul. Yahweh will forgive her.

9 "But the vow of a widow, or of her who is divorced, even everything with which she has bound her soul shall stand against her. **10** "If she vowed in her husband's house or bound her soul by a bond with an oath, **11** and her husband heard it, and didn't say anything to her, and didn't forbid her, then all her vows shall stand, **and every bond with which she bound her soul shall stand**. **12** But if her husband made them null and void in the day that he heard them, then whatever proceeded out of her lips concerning her vows, or concerning the bond of her soul, shall not stand. Her husband has made them void. Yahweh will forgive her.

30:13 Every vow, and every binding oath to afflict the soul, her husband may establish it, or her husband may make it void. **14** But if her husband says nothing to her from day to day, then he establishes all her vows or all her bonds which are on her. He has established them, because he said nothing to her in the day that he heard them. **15** But if he shall make them null and void after he has heard them, then he shall bear her iniquity."

16 These are the statutes which Yahweh commanded Moses, between a man and his wife, between a father and his daughter, being in her youth, in her father's house.

1Cor 14:40

Let **all things be done**

<u>decently</u>

and in **order**.

NOTE: [Matot.]

Numbers 31	1 Corinthians 14:40

Num 31:1 Yahweh spoke to Moses, saying, **2** "Avenge the children of Israel on the Midianites. Afterward you shall be gathered to your people." **3** Moses spoke to the people, saying, "**Arm men from among you for war, that they may go against Midian, to execute Yahweh's vengeance on Midian**. **4** You shall send one thousand out of every tribe of Israel to the war." **5** So there were delivered, out of the thousands of Israel, a thousand from every tribe, twelve thousand armed for war. **6** Moses sent them, one thousand of every tribe, to the war—them and Phinehas the son of Eleazar the priest—to the war, **with the vessels of the sanctuary and the trumpets for the alarm in his hand**. **7** They fought against Midian, as Yahweh commanded Moses. They killed every male. **8 They killed the kings of Midian with the rest of their slain: Evi, Rekem, Zur, Hur, and Reba, the five kings of Midian. They also killed Balaam the son of Beor with the sword**. **9** The children of Israel took the women of Midian captive with their little ones; and all their livestock, all their flocks, and all their goods, they took as plunder. **10** All their cities in the places where they lived, and all their encampments, they burned with fire. **11** They took all the captives, and all the plunder, both of man and of animal. **12** They brought the captives with the prey and the plunder, to Moses, and to Eleazar the priest, and to the congregation of the children of Israel, to the camp at the plains of Moab, which are by the Jordan at Jericho.

1Cor 14:40

Let all things be done

decently

and **in order**.

NOTE: After hearing God say to avenge the Children of Israel on the Midianites, Moses calls out to the people to fulfill the command. Moses does not modify or change it in any respect. . In this sense Moses is fulfilling "let *all things* be done." Once decided, Moses sends one thousand from every tribe, and Phinehas who would carry the vessels of the sanctuary and the trumpets for the alarm in his hand. The account does not state that God gave Moses these details, which strongly implies that Moses had determined these elements would fulfill God's command. This fulfills the idea of Moses letting "all things be done *decently*." Finally, in the fight, the killed "the five kings of Midian" who are all listed in a certain order, thus fulfilling "let all things be done decently and *in order*."

Num 31:13 Moses and Eleazar the priest, with all the princes of the congregation, went out to meet them outside of the camp. **14** Moses was angry with the officers of the army, the captains of thousands and the captains of hundreds, who came from the service of the war. **15** Moses said to them, "**Have you saved all the women alive**? **16 Behold, these caused the children of Israel, through the counsel of Balaam, to commit trespass against Yahweh in the matter of Peor, and so the plague was among the congregation of Yahweh**. **17** Now therefore kill every male among the little ones and kill every woman who has known man by lying with him. **18** But all the girls, who have not known man by lying with him, keep alive for yourselves. **19** "Encamp outside of the camp for seven days. Whoever has killed any person, and whoever has touched any slain, purify yourselves on the third day and on the seventh day, you and your captives. **20** As to every garment, and all that is made of skin, and all work of goats' hair, and all things made of wood, you shall purify yourselves."

21 Eleazar the priest said to the men of war who went to the battle, "This is the statute of the law which Yahweh has commanded Moses. **22** However the gold, and the silver, the brass, the iron, the tin, and the lead, **23** everything that may withstand the fire, you shall make to go through the fire, and it shall be clean; nevertheless it shall be purified with the water for impurity. All that doesn't withstand the fire you shall make to go through the water. **24** You shall wash your clothes on the seventh day, and you shall be clean. **Afterward you may come into the camp**."

1Cor 14:40

Let all things be done

decently

and **in order**.

NOTE: Here is a case of counter examples. "All the women were saved alive" was not all that Moses intended to be done! In fact, his explanation calls out the fact that it was just not an omission, but a trespass. Because of the trespass new commands were given, these being handled decently. Finally, to bring order Moses required them to encamp outside the camp for seven days before coming into the camp.

Num 31:25 Yahweh spoke to Moses, saying, **26** "**Count the plunder that was taken, both of man and of animal**, you, and Eleazar the priest, and the heads of the fathers' households of the congregation; **27** and <u>divide the plunder into two parts: between the men skilled in war, who went out to battle, and all the congregation</u>. **28** Levy a tribute to Yahweh of the men of war who went out to battle: **one soul of five hundred**; of the persons, of the cattle, of the donkeys, and of the flocks. **29** Take it from their half, and give it to Eleazar the priest, for Yahweh's wave offering. **30** Of the children of Israel's half, you shall take one drawn out of every fifty, of the persons, of the cattle, of the donkeys, and of the flocks, of all the livestock, and give them to the Levites, who perform the duty of the tabernacle of Yahweh." **31** Moses and Eleazar the priest did as Yahweh commanded Moses.

32 Now the prey, over and above the booty which the men of war took, was six hundred seventy-five thousand sheep, **33** seventy-two thousand head of cattle, **34** sixty-one thousand donkeys, **35** and thirty-two thousand persons in all, of the women who had not known man by lying with him.

36 The half, which was the portion of those who went out to war, was in number three hundred thirty-seven thousand five hundred sheep; **37** and Yahweh's tribute of the sheep was six hundred seventy-five. **38** The cattle were thirty-six thousand, of which Yahweh's tribute was seventy-two. **39** The donkeys were thirty thousand five hundred, of which Yahweh's tribute was sixty-one. **40** The persons were sixteen thousand of whom Yahweh's tribute was thirty-two persons. **41** Moses gave the tribute, which was Yahweh's wave offering, to Eleazar the priest, as Yahweh commanded Moses.

42 Of the children of Israel's half, which Moses divided off from the men who fought **43** (now the congregation's half was three hundred thirty-seven thousand five hundred sheep, **44** thirty-six thousand cattle, **45** thirty thousand five hundred donkeys, **46** and sixteen thousand persons), **47** even of the children of Israel's half, Moses took one drawn out of every fifty, both of man and of animal, and gave them to the Levites, who performed the duty of the tabernacle of Yahweh, as Yahweh commanded Moses.

1Cor 14:40

Let **all things be done**

<u>decently</u>

and in **order**.

NOTE: This passage details how "all things" were be done with regard to the distribution of the booty. This account seems to have been managed both decently and in order.

Num 31:48 The officers who were over the thousands of the army, the captains of thousands, and the captains of hundreds, came near to Moses. **49** They said to Moses, "Your servants have taken the sum of the men of war who are under our command, and **there lacks not one man of us**. 50 <u>We have brought Yahweh's offering, what every man found: gold ornaments, armlets, bracelets, signet rings, earrings, and necklaces, to make atonement for our souls before Yahweh</u>." **51** Moses and Eleazar the priest took their gold, even all worked jewels. **52** All the gold of the wave offering that they offered up to Yahweh, of the captains of thousands, and of the captains of hundreds, was sixteen thousand seven hundred fifty shekels. **53** The men of war had taken booty, every man for himself. **54 Moses and Eleazar the priest took the gold of the captains of thousands and of hundreds and brought it into the Tent of Meeting for a memorial for the children of Israel before Yahweh.**

1Cor 14:40

Let **all things be done**

<u>decently</u>

and in **order**.

NOTE: The manner of processing "what every man found" was also handled very well by the captains, Moses and the men.

Numbers 32	1 Corinthians 14:40

Num 32:1 Now the children of Reuben and the children of Gad had a very great multitude of livestock. They saw the land of Jazer, and the land of Gilead. Behold, the place was a place for livestock. **2** Then the children of Gad and the children of Reuben came and spoke to Moses, and to Eleazar the priest, and to the princes of the congregation, saying, **3** "Ataroth, Dibon, Jazer, Nimrah, Heshbon, Elealeh, Sebam, Nebo, and Beon, **4** the land which Yahweh struck before the congregation of Israel, is a land for livestock; and your servants have livestock." **5** They said, "If we have found favor in your sight, let this land be given to your servants for a possession. Don't bring us over the Jordan."

6 Moses said to the children of Gad, and to the children of Reuben, "Shall your brothers go to war while you sit here? **7** Why do you discourage the heart of the children of Israel from going over into the land which Yahweh has given them? **8** Your fathers did so when I sent them from Kadesh Barnea to see the land. **9** For when they went up to the valley of Eshcol, and saw the land, they discouraged the heart of the children of Israel, that they should not go into the land which Yahweh had given them. **10** Yahweh's anger burned in that day, and he swore, saying, **11** 'Surely none of the men who came up out of Egypt, from twenty years old and upward, shall see the land which I swore to Abraham, to Isaac, and to Jacob; because they have not wholly followed me, **12** except Caleb the son of Jephunneh the Kenizzite, and Joshua the son of Nun, because they have followed Yahweh completely.' **13** Yahweh's anger burned against Israel, and he made them wander back and forth in the wilderness forty years, until all the generation who had done evil in Yahweh's sight was consumed. **14** "Behold, you have risen up in your fathers' place, an increase of sinful men, to increase the fierce anger of Yahweh toward Israel. **15** For if you turn away from after him, he will yet again leave them in the wilderness; and you will destroy all this people."

1Cor 14:40 Let all things be done decently and in order.

(repeated)

NOTE: The echo applies categorically to all the verses in this pairing. Moses is very concerned that this desire from Reuben and Gad to take land east of the Jordan will cause all things *not* to be done, neither decently nor orderly. However, in the next pairing, the tribes will show good character in those very areas of Moses' concern.

Num 32:16 They came near to him, and said, "We will build sheepfolds here for our livestock, and cities for our little ones; **17** but we ourselves will be ready armed to go before the children of Israel, until we have brought them to their place. Our little ones shall dwell in the fortified cities because of the inhabitants of the land. **18 We will not return to our houses until the children of Israel have all received their inheritance**. 19 For <u>we will not inherit with them on the other side of the Jordan and beyond, because our inheritance has come to us on this side of the Jordan eastward</u>."

20 Moses said to them, "If you will do this thing, if you will arm yourselves to go before Yahweh to the war, **21** and every one of your armed men will pass over the Jordan before Yahweh until he has driven out his enemies from before him, **22** and the land is subdued before Yahweh; **then afterward you shall return, and be clear of obligation to Yahweh and to Israel**. Then this land shall be your possession before Yahweh. **23** "But if you will not do so, behold, you have sinned against Yahweh; and be sure your sin will find you out. **24** Build cities for your little ones, and folds for your sheep; and do that which has proceeded out of your mouth."

1Cor 14:40

Let all things be done

<u>decently</u>

and in **order**.

NOTE: Reuben and Gad begin to build their case for how their plan will not miss on any details and is both decent and orderly.

Num 32:25 The children of Gad and the children of Reuben spoke to Moses, saying, "Your servants will do as my lord commands. **26** Our little ones, our wives, our flocks, and **all** our livestock shall be there in the cities of Gilead; **27** but your servants will pass over, every man who is armed for war, before Yahweh to battle, as my lord says."

28 So Moses commanded concerning them to Eleazar the priest, and to Joshua the son of Nun, and to the heads of the fathers' households of the tribes of the children of Israel. **29** Moses said to them, "**If the children of Gad and the children of Reuben will pass with you over the Jordan, every man who is armed to battle before Yahweh, and the land is subdued before you, then you shall give them the land of Gilead for a possession**; **30** but if they will not pass over with you armed, they shall have possessions among you in the land of Canaan." **31** The children of Gad and the children of Reuben answered, saying, "As Yahweh has said to your servants, so will we do. **32 We will pass over armed before Yahweh into the land of Canaan, and the possession of our inheritance shall remain with us beyond the Jordan**."

33 Moses gave to them, even to the children of Gad, and to the children of Reuben, and to the half-tribe of Manasseh the son of Joseph, the kingdom of Sihon king of the Amorites, and the kingdom of Og king of Bashan; the land, according to its cities and borders, even the cities of the surrounding land. **34** The children of Gad built Dibon, Ataroth, Aroer, **35** Atroth-shophan, Jazer, Jogbehah, **36** Beth Nimrah, and Beth Haran: fortified cities and folds for sheep. **37** The children of Reuben built Heshbon, Elealeh, Kiriathaim, **38** Nebo, and Baal Meon, (their names being changed), and Sibmah. They gave other names to the cities which they built. **39** The children of Machir the son of Manasseh went to Gilead, took it, and dispossessed the Amorites who were therein. **40** Moses gave Gilead to Machir the son of Manasseh; and he lived therein. **41** Jair the son of Manasseh went and took its towns and called them Havvoth Jair. **42** Nobah went and took Kenath with its villages, and called it Nobah, after his own name.

1Cor 14:40

Let **all** things be done

decently

and in **order**.

NOTE: [Matot ends.] Reuben and Gad commit to carry out all the details of the plan, therefore Moses grants their request.

Numbers 33	1 Corinthians 15

Num 33:1 <u>**These are the journeys of the children of Israel, when they went out of the land of Egypt**</u> by their armies under the hand of Moses and Aaron. **2** Moses wrote the starting points of their journeys by the commandment of Yahweh. These are their journeys according to their starting points. **3** They traveled from Rameses in the first month, on the fifteenth day of the first month; on the next day after the Passover, the children of Israel went out with a high hand in the sight of all the Egyptians, **4** while the Egyptians were burying all their firstborn, whom Yahweh had struck among them. Yahweh also executed judgments on their gods.

1Cor 15:1a

Now <u>I</u> **<u>declare to you, brothers, the Good News</u>**

NOTE: [Masei.] The book of Numbers first summarizes the beginning of the journey, before listing the 42 stations of the Exodus. Paul also begins with a summary. Paul's "Good News" clearly echoes the Exodus from land of Egypt.

Num 33:5 The children of Israel traveled from Rameses and <u>encamped in Succoth</u>. **6** They traveled from Succoth, and **<u>encamped in Etham</u>**, which is in the edge of the wilderness. **7** They traveled from Etham, and <u>turned back to Pihahiroth</u>, which is before Baal Zephon, and they encamped before Migdol. **8** They traveled from Pihahiroth and passed through the middle of the sea into the wilderness. They went **three days' journey in the wilderness of Etham and encamped in Marah**. **9** They traveled from Marah and <u>came to Elim</u>. In Elim, there were twelve springs of water and seventy palm trees, and they encamped there. **10** They traveled from Elim and **encamped by the Red Sea**. **11** They traveled from the Red Sea and encamped in the <u>wilderness of Sin</u>.

1Cor 15:1b which I <u>preached</u> to you, which also you <u>received</u>, in which you also <u>stand</u>, **2** by which also you are <u>saved</u>, if you <u>hold</u> firmly the word which I **preached** to you—unless you <u>believed</u> in vain.

NOTE: This section lists first seven stations: 1-7 of a list of the **42 stations** of the Exodus echoing verbs 1-7 of the **42 verbs** Paul associates with the Good News of the work of Jesus.

Num 33:12 They traveled from the wilderness of Sin and encamped in Dophkah. **13** They traveled from Dophkah and encamped in Alush. **14** They traveled from Alush, and encamped in **Rephidim, where there was no water for the people to drink**. **15** They traveled from Rephidim and encamped in the wilderness of Sinai. **16** They traveled from the wilderness of Sinai and encamped in Kibroth Hattaavah.

1**Cor 15:3** For I delivered to you first of all that which I also received: that Christ **died** for our sins according to the Scriptures, **4** that he was buried, that he was raised on the third day according to the Scriptures,

NOTE: The next five echoes: 8-12. Notice how Numbers specifically calls out the dire situation at Rephidim.

Num 33:17 They traveled from Kibroth Hattaavah and encamped in Hazeroth. **18** They traveled from Hazeroth and encamped in Rithmah. **19** They traveled from Rithmah and encamped in **Rimmon Perez**. **20** They traveled from Rimmon Perez and encamped in Libnah. **21** They traveled from Libnah and encamped in Rissah. **22** They traveled from Rissah and encamped in **Kehelathah**. **23** They traveled from Kehelathah and encamped in Mount Shepher. **24** They traveled from Mount Shepher and encamped in Haradah. **25** They traveled from Haradah and encamped in **Makheloth**. **26** They traveled from Makheloth and encamped in Tahath. **27** They traveled from Tahath and encamped in Terah. **28** They traveled from Terah and encamped in **Mithkah**. **29** They traveled from Mithkah and encamped in Hashmonah.

1**Cor 15:5** and that he appeared to Cephas, then to the twelve. **6** Then he appeared to over five hundred brothers at once, most of whom **remain** until now, but some have also fallen asleep. **7** Then he appeared to James, then to all the apostles, **8** and last of all, as to the child **born** at the wrong time, he appeared to me also. **9** For I am the least of the apostles, who is not worthy to be called an apostle, because I **persecuted** the assembly of God. **10** But by the grace of God I am what I am. His grace which was given to me was not futile, but I worked more than all of them; yet not I, but the grace of God which was with me. **11** Whether then it is I or they, so we **preach**, and so you believed.

NOTE: The next thirteen echoes: 13-25.

Num 33:30 They traveled from Hashmonah and encamped in <u>Moseroth</u>. **31** They traveled from Moseroth and encamped in <u>Bene Jaakan</u>. **32** They traveled from Bene Jaakan and encamped in **<u>Hor Haggidgad</u>**. **33** They traveled from Hor Haggidgad and encamped in <u>Jotbathah</u>. **34** They traveled from Jotbathah and encamped in <u>Abronah</u>. **35** They traveled from Abronah and encamped in <u>Ezion Geber</u>. **36** They traveled from Ezion Geber and encamped at **<u>Kadesh</u>** in the wilderness of Zin. **37** They traveled from Kadesh, and encamped in <u>Mount Hor</u>, in the edge of the land of Edom.

1**Cor 15:12** Now if Christ is <u>preached</u>, that he has been <u>raised</u> from the dead, how do some among you **<u>say</u>** that there is no resurrection of the dead? **13** But if there is no resurrection of the dead, neither has Christ been <u>raised</u>. **14** If Christ has not been <u>raised</u>, then our preaching is in vain, and your faith also is in vain. **15** Yes, we are also <u>found</u> false witnesses of God, because we **<u>testified</u>** about God that he <u>raised</u> up Christ,

NOTE: The next eight echoes: 26-33.

Num 33:38 Aaron the priest went up into Mount Hor at the commandment of Yahweh, and died there, in the fortieth year after the children of Israel had come out of the land of Egypt, in the fifth month, on the first day of the month. **39** Aaron was one hundred twenty-three years old when he died in Mount Hor. **40** The Canaanite king of Arad, who lived in the South in the land of Canaan, heard of the coming of the children of Israel.

NOTE: In an effort to complete the list of 42 aspects of Christ's resurrection, Paul seems to skip these verses momentarily but return to them after the next pairing.

Num 33:41 They traveled from Mount Hor and encamped in <u>Zalmonah</u>. **42** They traveled from Zalmonah and encamped in <u>Punon</u>. **43** They traveled from Punon and encamped in <u>Oboth</u>. **44** They traveled from Oboth, and encamped in <u>Iye Abarim</u>, in the border of Moab. **45** They traveled from Iyim and encamped in <u>Dibon Gad</u>. **46** They traveled from Dibon Gad and encamped in <u>Almon Diblathaim</u>. **47** They traveled from Almon Diblathaim, and encamped in the mountains of Abarim, before <u>Nebo</u>. **48** They traveled from the mountains of Abarim and encamped in the <u>plains of Moab</u> by the Jordan at Jericho. **49** They encamped <u>by the Jordan</u>, from Beth Jeshimoth even to Abel Shittim in the plains of Moab.

1Cor 15:15b

whom he didn't <u>raise</u> up if it is true that the dead are not <u>raised</u>. **16** For if the dead aren't <u>raised</u>, neither has Christ been <u>raised</u>. **17** If Christ has not been <u>raised</u>, your faith is vain; you are still in your sins. **18** Then they also who are <u>fallen asleep</u> in Christ have <u>perished</u>. **19** If we have only <u>hoped</u> in Christ in this life, we are of all men most <u>pitiable</u>.

NOTE: The last nine echoes. 34-42. An analysis of the meanings of the various stations of the Exodus would surely yield greater understanding of Paul's choice of words in those cases.

Num 33:38 Aaron the **priest went up** into Mount Hor at the commandment of Yahweh, and **died there**, in the fortieth year after the **children of Israel had come out of the land of Egypt**, in the fifth month, on the first day of the month. **39** <u>**Aaron was one hundred twenty-three years old when he died**</u> in Mount Hor. **40** The Canaanite king of Arad, who lived in the South in the land of Canaan, **heard of the coming** of the <u>**children of Israel**</u>.

1Cor 15:20 But now **Christ has been raised** from the dead. He became the first fruit of <u>**those who are asleep**</u>. **21** For since death came by man, the resurrection of the dead also came by man. **22** For as in Adam all die, so also **in Christ all will be made alive**. **23** <u>**But each in his own order**</u>: Christ the first fruit, **then those who are Christ's at his coming**. **24** Then the end comes, when he will deliver up <u>**the Kingdom to God**</u>, even the Father, when he will have abolished all rule and all authority and power.

NOTE: Paul now goes back to the three verses he skipped and uses the death of Aaron to speak to the resurrection from the dead of all the saints.

Num 33:50 Yahweh spoke to Moses in the plains of Moab by the Jordan at **Jericho**, saying, **51** "Speak to the children of Israel, and tell them, '**When you pass over the Jordan into the land of Canaan**, **33:52** then you shall *drive out all the inhabitants of the land* from before you, destroy all their stone idols, destroy all their molten images, and demolish all their high places. **53 You shall take possession of the land, and dwell therein**; for I have given the land to you to possess it.

1Cor 15:25 For he must reign until he has put all his enemies under his feet. **26** The last enemy that will be abolished is death. **27** For, "He put all things in subjection under his feet." But when he says, "All things are put in subjection," it is evident that he is excepted who subjected all things to him. **28** When all things have been subjected to him, then the Son will also himself be subjected to him who subjected all things to him, that God may be all in all.

15:29 Or else what will they do who are baptized for the dead? If the dead aren't raised at all, why then are they baptized for the dead? **30** Why do we also stand in jeopardy every hour? **31** I affirm, by the boasting in you which I have in Christ Jesus our Lord, I die daily. **32** If **I** *fought with animals at Ephesus* for human purposes, what does it profit me? If the dead are not raised, then "let's eat and drink, for tomorrow we die." **33** Don't be deceived! "Evil companionships corrupt good morals." **34 Wake up righteously, and don't sin**, for some have no knowledge of God. I say this to your shame.

NOTE: The first echo is proposed because the walls came down so that Israel could enter on foot. 1 Corinthians 15:29 is a verse on which much has been written, and its proposed echo into Numbers while somewhat fitting, does not add much to the discussion. 1 Cor. 15:32 is clearly speaking of human beings, thus the echo is also to human beings.

Num 33:54 You shall inherit the land by lot according to your families; to the larger groups you shall give a larger inheritance, and to the smaller you shall give a smaller inheritance. Wherever the lot falls to any man, that shall be his. You shall inherit according to the tribes of your fathers. **55** "'But if you do not drive out the inhabitants of the land from before you, then those you let remain of them will be like pricks in your eyes and thorns in your sides. They will harass you in the land in which you dwell. **56** It shall happen that as I thought to do to them, so I will do to you.'"

1Cor 15:35 But someone will say, "How are the dead raised?" and, "With what kind of body do they come?" **36** You foolish one, that which you yourself sow is not made alive unless it dies. **37** That which you sow, you don't sow the body that will be, but a bare grain, maybe of wheat, or of some other kind. **38** But God gives it a body even as it pleased him, and to each seed a body of its own. **39** All flesh is not the same flesh, but there is one flesh of men, another flesh of animals, another of fish, and another of birds. **40** There are also celestial bodies and terrestrial bodies; but the glory of the celestial differs from that of the terrestrial. **41** There is one glory of the sun, another glory of the moon, and another glory of the stars; for one star differs from another star in glory.

42 So also is the resurrection of the dead. The body is sown perishable; it is raised imperishable. **43** It is sown in dishonor; it is raised in glory. It is sown in weakness; it is raised in power. **44** It is sown a natural body; it is raised a spiritual body. There is a natural body and there is also a spiritual body. **45** So also it is written, "The first man, Adam, became a living soul." The last Adam became a life-giving spirit. **46** However that which is spiritual isn't first, but that which is natural, then that which is spiritual. **47** The first man is of the earth, made of dust. The second man is the Lord from heaven. **48** As is the one made of dust, such are those who are also made of dust; and as is the heavenly, such are they also that are heavenly. **49** As we have borne the image of those made of dust, let's also bear the image of the heavenly.

NOTE: The echo between these two sides is a metaphor. God promised Israel that they will cross over the Jordan and will inherit the land by lot according to their families. This traversing the Jordan "in a sense a baptism" echoes Paul's explanation of the eventual resurrection from the dead. Paul writes "The body is sown perishable; it is raised imperishable." Paul may be considering that Moses and Aaron died before crossing into the promised land, so their inheritance of that land is a spiritual one. After they drive out the inhabitants of the land, the land of Israel will be of a higher glory than that of Canaan.

| Numbers 34 | 1 Cor. 15:50 |

Num 34:1 Yahweh spoke to Moses, saying, **2** "Command the children of Israel, and tell them, 'When you come into the land of Canaan (**this is the land that shall fall to you for an inheritance**, even the land of Canaan according to its borders), **3** then your south quarter shall be from the wilderness of Zin along by the side of Edom, and your south border shall be from the end of the Salt Sea eastward. **4** Your border shall turn about southward of the ascent of Akrabbim and pass along to Zin; and it shall pass southward of Kadesh Barnea; and it shall go from there to Hazar Addar, and pass along to Azmon. **5** The border shall turn about from Azmon to the brook of Egypt, and it shall end at the sea.

6 "'For the western border, you shall have the great sea and its coast. This shall be your west border.

7 "'This shall be your north border: from the great sea you shall mark out for you Mount Hor; **8** from Mount Hor you shall mark out to the entrance of Hamath; and the border shall pass by Zedad. **9** Then the border shall go to Ziphron, and it shall end at Hazar Enan. This shall be your north border.

10 "'You shall mark out your east border from Hazar Enan to Shepham. **11** The border shall go down from Shepham to Riblah, on the east side of Ain. The border shall go down and shall reach to the side of the sea of Chinnereth eastward. **12** The border shall go down to the Jordan, and its end shall be at the Salt Sea. This shall be your land according to its borders around it.'"

13 Moses commanded the **children of Israel, saying, "This is the land which you shall inherit** by lot, which Yahweh has commanded to give to the nine tribes, and to the half-tribe; **14** for the tribe of the children of Reuben according to their fathers' houses, the tribe of the children of Gad according to their fathers' houses, and the half-tribe of Manasseh have received their inheritance. **15** The two tribes and the half-tribe have received their inheritance **beyond the Jordan at Jericho eastward, toward the sunrise**."

1**Cor 15:50** Now I say this, brothers, that **flesh and blood can't inherit God's Kingdom**; neither does the perishable inherit imperishable. **51** Behold, I tell you a mystery. We will not all sleep, but **we will all be changed**, **52** in a moment, **in the twinkling of an eye, at the last trumpet. For the trumpet will sound** and the dead will be raised incorruptible, and we will be changed.

NOTE: While these echoes are interesting they add little to Paul's interpretation. Indeed, a trumpet did sound at Jericho.

Num 34:16 Yahweh spoke to Moses, saying, **17** "These are the **names of the men** who shall divide the land to you for inheritance: Eleazar the priest, and **Joshua the son of Nun**. **18** You shall take **one prince of every tribe**, to divide the land for inheritance. **19** These are the names of the men: Of the tribe of Judah, Caleb the son of Jephunneh. **20** Of the tribe of the children of Simeon, Shemuel the son of Ammihud. **21** Of the tribe of Benjamin, Elidad the son of Chislon. **22** Of the tribe of the children of Dan a prince, Bukki the son of Jogli. **23** Of the children of Joseph: of the tribe of the children of Manasseh a prince, Hanniel the son of Ephod. **24** Of the tribe of the children of Ephraim a prince, Kemuel the son of Shiphtan. **25** Of the tribe of the children of Zebulun a prince, Elizaphan the son of Parnach. **26** Of the tribe of the children of Issachar a prince, Paltiel the son of Azzan. **27** Of the tribe of the children of Asher a prince, Ahihud the son of Shelomi. **28** Of the tribe of the children of Naphtali a prince, Pedahel the son of Ammihud." **29** These are they whom Yahweh commanded to *divide the inheritance to the children of Israel in the land of Canaan*.

1Cor 15:53 For this

perishable body must become imperishable, and this mortal must put on immortality. **54** But when this perishable body will have become imperishable, and this mortal will have put on immortality, then what is written will happen: "Death is swallowed up in victory." **55** "Death, where is your sting? Hades, where is your victory?" **56** The sting of death is sin, and the power of sin is the law. **57** But thanks be to God, who gives us the **victory through our Lord Jesus Christ**.

58 Therefore,

my **beloved brothers**, be steadfast, immovable, always abounding in the Lord's work, because you know that **your labor is not in vain in the Lord**.

NOTE: After the statement "one prince of every tribe" the section lists the word "prince" seven more times, and the word "tribe" ten more times.

Numbers 35	1 Corinthians 16

Num 35:1 Yahweh spoke to Moses in the plains of Moab by the Jordan at Jericho, saying, **2** "Command the children of Israel to give to the Levites cities to dwell in out of their inheritance. **You shall give pasture lands for the cities around them to the Levites**. **3** They shall have the cities to dwell in. Their pasture lands shall be for their livestock, and for their possessions, and for all their animals.

4 "The pasture lands of the cities, which you shall give to the Levites, shall be from the wall of the city and outward one thousand cubits around it. **5** You shall measure outside of the city for the east side two thousand cubits, and for the south side two thousand cubits, and for the west side two thousand cubits, and for the north side two thousand cubits, the city being in the middle. This shall be the pasture lands of their cities.

6 "The cities which you shall give to the Levites, they shall be the six cities of refuge, which you shall give for the manslayer to flee to. Besides them you shall give forty-two cities. **7** All the cities which you shall give to the Levites shall be forty-eight cities together with their pasture lands. **8** Concerning the cities which you shall give of the possession of the children of Israel, **from the many you shall take many, and from the few you shall take few**. Everyone according to his inheritance which he inherits shall *give* some of his cities to the Levites."

1Cor 16:1 Now concerning the

collection for the saints: as I commanded the assemblies of Galatia, you do likewise.

2 On the first day of every week, let each one of you save, as he may prosper, that no collections are made when I come. **3** When I arrive, I will send whoever you approve with letters to carry your gracious *gift* to Jerusalem. **4** If it is appropriate for me to go also, they will go with me.

NOTE: The echo of "collection for the saints" could also potentially be "give the Levites cities," in Numbers 35:2.

Num 35:9 Yahweh spoke to Moses, saying, **10** "Speak to the children of Israel, and tell them, 'When you pass over the Jordan into the land of Canaan, **11** then you shall appoint for yourselves cities to be cities of refuge for you, that the manslayer who kills any person unwittingly may flee there. **12** The cities shall be for your refuge from the avenger, that the manslayer not die until he stands before the congregation for judgment. **13** The cities which you shall give shall be for you six cities of refuge. **14** You shall give **three cities beyond the Jordan**, and you shall give *three cities in the land of Canaan*. They shall be cities of refuge. **15** These six cities shall be for refuge for the children of Israel, for the stranger, and for the foreigner living among them, that everyone who kills any person unwittingly may flee there.

1Cor 16:5 But I will <u>**come**</u> to you when I have **passed** through Macedonia, for I am **passing** through Macedonia. **6** But with you it may be that I will *stay*, or even winter, that you may *send* me on my journey wherever I *go*.

NOTE: The three verbs in 1 Corinthians 16:5, *come*, *passed*, and *passing* speak of faraway places and may echo the three cities beyond the Jordan. The three verbs in 1 Cor. 16:6, *stay*, *send* and *go*, speak of being with them, and may echo the three cities in the promised land of Canaan. Apparently, for Paul, being present with the people of God is his refuge as explained more in the next pairing.

Num 35:16 "'But if he struck him with an instrument of iron, so that he died, he is a murderer. The murderer shall surely be put to death. **17** If he struck him with a stone in the hand, by which a man may die, and he died, he is a murderer. The murderer shall surely be put to death. **18** Or if he struck him with a weapon of wood in the hand, by which a man may die, and he died, he is a murderer. The murderer shall surely be put to death. **19** The avenger of blood shall himself put the murderer to death. **When he meets him,** he shall put him to death. **20** If he shoved him out of hatred, or hurled something at him while lying in wait, so that he died, **21** or in hostility struck him with his hand, so that he died, he who struck him shall surely be put to death. He is a murderer. The avenger of blood shall put the murderer to death when he meets him.

22 "'But if he shoved him suddenly without hostility, or hurled on him anything without lying in wait, **23** or with any stone, by which a man may die, not seeing him, and cast it on him so that he died, and he was not his enemy and not seeking his harm, **24** then the congregation shall judge between the striker and the avenger of blood according to these ordinances. **25** The congregation shall deliver the manslayer out of the hand of the avenger of blood, and the congregation shall **restore him to his city of refuge where he had fled**. He shall dwell therein **until** the death of the high priest, who was anointed with the holy oil. **26** "'But if the manslayer shall at any time go beyond the border of **his city of refuge where he flees**, **27** and **the avenger of blood finds him outside of the border of his city of refuge**, and the avenger of blood kills the manslayer, he shall not be guilty of blood, **28** because he should have remained in his city of refuge until the death of the high priest. But after the death of the high priest, the manslayer shall return into the land of his possession.

1Cor 16:7 For **I do not wish to see you now in passing**, but I hope to stay a while with you, if the Lord permits. **8 But I will stay at Ephesus** until Pentecost, **9** for a great and effective *door has opened to me*, and **there are many adversaries**.

NOTE: Here the "door" is the door <u>into</u> Ephesus, the city of refuge. Paul alludes to the avenger in his speaking of his having many adversaries. No explanation has been found between the timing of Paul's visit (staying until Pentecost / Shavuot), and its echo, the manslayer needing to wait until the death of the high priest.

Num 35:29 "'These things shall be for a statute and ordinance to you throughout your generations in all your dwellings. **30** "'Whoever kills any person, the murderer shall be slain at the mouth of witnesses; but one witness shall not testify against any person that he die. **31** "'Moreover you shall take no ransom for the life of a murderer who is guilty of death. He shall surely be put to death. **32** "'You shall take no ransom for him who has fled to his city of refuge, that he may come again to dwell in the land before the death of the priest. **33** "'So you shall not pollute the land where you are. For blood pollutes the land. No atonement can be made for the land for the blood that is shed in it, but by the blood of him who shed it. **34** You shall not defile the land which you inhabit, in the middle of which I dwell; for I, Yahweh, dwell among the children of Israel.'"

NOTE: Paul appears to skip these verses.

Numbers 36	1 Corinthians 16:10

Num 36:1 The heads of the fathers' households of the family of the children of Gilead, the son of Machir, the son of Manasseh, of the families of the **sons of Joseph, came** near, and **spoke before Moses, and before the princes**, the heads of the fathers' households of the children of Israel. **2** They said, "Yahweh commanded my lord to give the land for inheritance by lot to the children of Israel. My lord was commanded by Yahweh to give the inheritance of Zelophehad our **brother** to his daughters.	1**Cor 16:10** Now if **Timothy comes**, see that he is with you without fear, **for he does the work of the Lord**, as I also do. **11** Therefore let no one despise him. But set him forward on his journey in peace, that he may come to me; for I expect him with the **brothers**.
Num 36:3 If they are married to any of the **sons of the other tribes of the children of Israel**, then their inheritance will be **taken away** from the inheritance of our fathers and will be added to the inheritance of the tribe to which they belong. So, it will be taken away from the lot of our inheritance.	1**Cor 16:12** But **concerning Apollos**, the brother, I strongly urged him to come to you with the brothers; and **it was not at all his desire to come now**; but he will come when he has an opportunity.

NOTE: While Apollos is Paul's brother in the Lord, he is not working directly with Paul. This echoes "sons of the *other* tribes...." This designation finds support in 1 Corinthians 1:12. The fact that Apollos does not want to "come now" is not a slight on him, according to the echo since Apollos' inheritance will first be according to those areas in which Apollos was called by God.

Num 36:4 <u>When the jubilee of the children of Israel comes, then their inheritance will be added to the inheritance of the tribe to which they belong</u>. *So, their inheritance will be taken away from the inheritance of the tribe of our fathers.*"

36:5 Moses commanded the children of Israel according to Yahweh's word, saying, "The tribe of the sons of Joseph speaks right. **6** This is the thing which Yahweh commands concerning the daughters of Zelophehad, saying, '<u>Let them be married to whom they think best, only they shall marry into the family of the tribe of their father</u>.

1Cor 16:13 <u>Watch! Stand firm in the faith</u>! *Be courageous! Be strong!* **14** <u>Let all that you do be done in love</u>.

NOTE: Given the pressure the women might be under to marry into the family of their father, Paul's command is especially relevant. It is possible for a person to do the right *things*, but not the right *way*.

Num 36:7 So shall no inheritance of the **children** of Israel remove from tribe to tribe; for the children of Israel shall each hold to the inheritance of the **tribe of his fathers**. **8** Every daughter who possesses an inheritance in any tribe of the children of Israel shall be wife to one of the family of the tribe of her father, <u>that the children of Israel may each possess the inheritance of his fathers</u>. **9** So shall no inheritance remove from one tribe to another tribe; for the tribes of the children of Israel shall each hold to his own inheritance."

1Cor 16:15 Now I beg you, **brothers**— you know the **house of Stephanas**, that it is the first fruits of Achaia, and that they have set themselves to serve the saints— **16** that you also **be in subjection to such, and to everyone who helps in the work and labors**. **17** I rejoice at the coming of Stephanas, Fortunatus, and Achaicus; for that which was lacking on your part, they supplied. **18** For they refreshed my spirit and yours. Therefore, acknowledge those who are like that.

NOTE: Just as should happen within a specific tribe of Israel, Paul seems to be saying that since Achaia is the province in which Corinth resides, that the household of Stephanas should be considered worthy of respect and collaboration, as "one of their own."

Num 36:10 So the daughters of Zelophehad did as Yahweh commanded Moses. **11** For Mahlah, Tirzah, Hoglah, Milcah, and Noah, the daughters of Zelophehad, were married to their father's brothers' sons. **12** <u>They were married into the families of the sons of Manasseh the son of Joseph</u>. Their inheritance remained in the tribe of the family of their father.

1Cor 16:19 The assemblies of Asia greet you. **Aquila and Priscilla** greet you warmly in the Lord, together with the assembly that is in their house. **20** All the brothers greet you. Greet one another with a holy kiss.

NOTE: Even though the women of Zelophehad were strong, they chose to marry into their own tribe. Similarly, while Priscilla is a strong woman, Paul lists Aquila's name first, establishing the marriage order. In every other biblical mention after their introduction in Acts 18:2, including every other mention by Paul, her name is listed first (Acts 18:18, 26, Romans 16:3, 2 Timothy 4:19).

Num 36:13 These are the commandments and the ordinances which Yahweh commanded by **Moses** to the children of Israel in the plains of **Moab by the Jordan** at Jericho.	**1Cor 16:21** This greeting is by me, **Paul**, with my own hand. **22** If any man doesn't love the Lord Jesus Christ, let him be cursed. **Come, Lord!**

NOTE: [Masei ends.] Paul's phrase "Come, Lord!," or maranatha in the Greek, echoes the phrase "Moab by the Jordan" which literally means "of the father who descends"! Regarding the unusual statement from Paul in 1 Corinthians 16:22, "If any man doesn't love the Lord Jesus Christ, let him be cursed," two main echo possibilities exist. First, Paul may have been thinking back to Balak, who, while he did not actually curse Israel, tried to pay Balaam to do it. If true, Paul might be adding a thought he was looking to work in earlier in his letter but never found the opportunity. A second, possibility is that Paul may have been thinking of Joshua as a picture of Christ, who is about to lead God's people against Jericho. In the book of Joshua, after conquering Jericho he will famously declare "cursed before the Lord is anyone who tries to rebuild this city!" Centuries later, in 1 Kings 16:34, Hiel from Bethel tried to rebuild it and was cursed. Paul may have recognized in Hiel a lack of love of, and even defiance of his forefather Joshua, and therefore Hiel, at least spiritually, was in *defiance* of Jesus Christ.

The Book of Numbers	**1Cor 16:23** The grace of the Lord Jesus Christ be with you. **24** My love to all of you in Christ Jesus. Amen.

NOTE: The last two verses of 1 Corinthians seem to summarize the entire letter to the Corinthians and echo the entire book of Numbers. God was with His people in their entire journey, and the love of Christ was active and present in their entire journey, even if his presence was hidden.

NOTE: Paul's second letter to the Corinthians echoes the book of Deuteronomy. Both of these books, immediately following the preceding verses, are explored in Vol. V of the Echoes Bible series.

THE STORY OF THE ECHOES BIBLE

The discovery of the ancient connections between Paul's New Testament letters and the Old Testament books was made by John David Pitcher in 2008. He has published material on these connections under the title *The Oldest Midrash*. His discoveries were made primarily through linguistic analysis of the Septuagint in comparison with the New Testament. For more information see echoesbible.org/john-david-pitcher/.

When Bob O'Dell first learned of David's discoveries, he began to examine them carefully to determine whether the claims were true. David asserted in 2015 that six of Paul's epistles connected to major books of the Old Testament: Genesis to Hebrews, Exodus to Galatians, Leviticus to Romans, Numbers to 2 Timothy, Deuteronomy to 1 Timothy, and Joshua to Titus—discoveries made between 2008 and 2012. Once learning of the discovery, Bob devoted nine months to studying David's assertions in the first three pairings listed above, declaring David's discoveries to be valid. Bob found that, although he already considered himself skilled in "seeing Jesus in every page of the Old Testament," it nevertheless required time to begin perceiving those passages in the same light in which Paul himself had seen them. Paul saw far more, and Bob had to learn how Paul approached those texts—an approach that was both deeper and, at times, more obvious than he expected. It was as though, after many years of Bible study, Bob was reading the Scriptures again for the first time. Yet it was not that the truth itself was new, for Paul's words had not changed. Rather, the primary insight lay in the beauty and awe of how Paul conceptualized the Old Testament texts within the life of ancient Israel. The work of Christ was fully prefigured! It is no wonder that Paul would declare that all Scripture is useful for doctrine.

Over the next five years, with new eyes to perceive Paul's writings, Bob O'Dell combined linguistic analysis with thematic resonance, thereby both deepening the connections identified in David's discoveries and making additional, as yet unpublished discoveries as well. Whereas David has focused on the midrashic aspect of Paul's literary decisions within the academic realm, Bob has concentrated on the echoes between the Testaments— showing how each text further contextualizes and illuminates the other. His desire was that serious Bible students around the world might experience what he himself experienced: to be filled with awe and wonder at God, His Word, and the finished work of His Son. This has led to the formation of the Echoes Bible Foundation, a U.S. based 501(c)3 organization whose mission is to disseminate these insights both in print and online. Bob and David remain close friends.

The World English Bible (WEB) is used for the text due to its non-copyright status. The Echoes Bible Foundation considers the decision by eBible.org to publish a non-copyrighted modern English version of the Bible based on the non-copyrighted *New American Standard 1901*, to be a magnificent gift to the modern world.

For more on the Echoes Bible see echoesbible.org or echoesbible.com.